Green Line 5

Standardaufgaben

von
Jennifer Baer-Engel
Elizabeth Daymond
Dieter Firmenich
Miriam Firmenich
Dr. Uta von Reinersdorff

Ernst Klett Verlag
Stuttgart • Leipzig

Green Line 5 Standardaufgaben

Autorinnen: Elizabeth Daymond M. A., Kiel; Dieter und Miriam Firmenich, Duisburg; Dr. Uta von Reinersdorff, Herford, sowie Jennifer Baer-Engel, Göppingen

Beraterin: Beate Günther, Hannover

Zeichenerklärung:

◎ Übungen mit diesem Symbol verweisen auf die Audio-Tracks.

Bildquellenverzeichnis:
Cov1; Cov4 Getty Images (Digital Vision), München; **8.1** Klett-Archiv (Patrick Ward), Stuttgart; **8.2** Ullstein Bild GmbH (TopFoto), Berlin; **11.1** Avenue Images GmbH RF (Corbis RF), Hamburg; **11.2** Alamy Images (Travel-Shots), Abingdon, Oxon; **11.3** Corbis (Free Agents Limited), Düsseldorf; **11.4** Corbis (Hans Reinhard), Düsseldorf; **11.5** Dream Maker Software (RF), Colorado; **11.6** iStockphoto (resonants), Calgary, Alberta; **11.7** iStockphoto (xyno), Calgary, Alberta; **18.1** Getty Images (Lisa Maree Williams), München; **24.1** Getty Images (Image Bank/AlanThornton), München; **24.2** Avenue Images GmbH RF (Brand X pictures), Hamburg; **31.1; 31.2; 31.3** Klett-Archiv (Patrick Ward), Stuttgart; **37.1** GOODSHOOT (Goodshoot), Annecy-Le-Vieux; **41.1; 41.2; 41.3; 41.4; 41.5; 41.6** Klett-Archiv (Patrick Ward), Stuttgart; **43.1** Oxfam Deutschland e.V. (Justin Sutcliffe), Berlin; **43.2** Corbis (Barry Lewis), Düsseldorf; **43.3** Getty Images (LUIS LIWANAG/AFP), München; **43.4** laif (Marie Dorigny), Köln; **44.1** Getty Images (Michael Ochs Archives), München; **48.1** Corbis (Robert van der Hilst), Düsseldorf;

Nicht in allen Fällen war es uns möglich, den Rechteinhaber der Abbildungen ausfindig zu machen. Berechtigte Ansprüche werden selbstverständlich im Rahmen der üblichen Vereinbarungen abgegolten.

1. Auflage 1 5 4 3 2 1 | 2013 12 11 10 09

Internetadresse: www.klett.de

Redaktion: Lektorat editoria, Cornelia Schaller, Fellbach
Herstellung: Anne Leibbrand

Illustrationen: Simone Pahl, Berlin
Umschlaggestaltung: Koma Amok, Stuttgart
Reproduktion: Meyle + Müller, Medien-Management, Pforzheim
Satz: Jacqueline Köhler
Druck: Medienhaus Plump, Rheinbreitbach

Printed in Germany
ISBN 978-3-12-547164-1

9 783125 471641

CD-ROM

Diesem Arbeitsheft liegt Software bei. Die Urheber und Mitwirkenden sind den entsprechenden Verzeichnissen auf der CD-ROM zu entnehmen.
Sollten Sie Probleme mit dem vorliegenden Programm haben, finden Sie in der Datei „Hotline.txt", die sich auf der obersten Ebene der CD-ROM befindet, unsere Kontaktdaten und weitere Hilfestellungen.

Audio-CD

Aufnahmeleitung: Ernst Klett Verlag GmbH, Stuttgart
Redaktion: Lektorat editoria, Cornelia Schaller, Fellbach
Tonaufnahme: Joseph Degnan at The Audio Workshop, London
Produktion: Andrew Branch for RBA Productions, London
Sprecherinnen und Sprecher:
Elaine Claxton, Jane Collingwood, Rupert Farley, Wayne Forrester, Nigel Greaves, Nicola Hornet, Harriet Kershaw, Kristopher Milnes, Nigel Pilkington, Chris Rowe, Jane Whittenshaw

Presswerk: OK Medien Service, Boizenburg / Elbe

Gesamtzeit: 30'43"

Inhalt

Liebe Lehrerin, lieber Lehrer,

die Lehrplananforderungen legen immer mehr Wert auf Kompetenzorientierung und einen kommunikativen Ansatz der Aufgaben. Bei den *Green Line* 5 Standardaufgaben haben wir diese Anforderungen wieder optimal umgesetzt. Dieses Heft bietet Ihnen Aufgaben, die auf dem neuesten Stand sind und daher für Sie noch besser zum Erstellen von Klassenarbeiten nach Kompetenzen geeignet sind.

Aufbau der Standardaufgaben im Überblick

Die Units bestehen jeweils aus zwei Teilen:

Im **Kompetenzteil** (auf den ersten 5–6 Seiten jeder Unit) finden Sie Aufgaben zu den kommunikativen Kompetenzen Hörverstehen, kombiniertes Hör-/Sehverstehen (*Understanding films*), Leseverstehen, Schreiben, Sprechen und Sprachmittlung.
Bei der Entwicklung der kompetenzorientierten Aufgaben wurde besonderen Wert auf Einbettung in für die Schüler alltagstaugliche Situationen und kommunikativen Anspruch gelegt.
Obwohl das Überprüfen der Kompetenz Sprechen nicht wie die übrigen Kompetenzen Bestandteil der herkömmlichen Leistungskontrolle ist, soll die Aufnahme dieser Aufgabenvorschläge in das Heft jedoch als Ermunterung verstanden werden, solche Formate bei der Leistungsfeststellung einzusetzen.

Die **Aufgaben zur Abfrage von spezifischen sprachlichen Mitteln** finden Sie im zweiten Teil der Units (5–6 Seiten jeweils).
Auch bei diesen Testformaten wurde größtenteils darauf geachtet, dass sie situativ eingebettet sind und eine kommunikative Absicht verfolgen. Die Aufgaben bieten Ihnen jedoch die Möglichkeit, das Verständnis einzelner sprachlicher Phänomene gezielt zu überprüfen.

Wir freuen uns, Ihnen diese neuen *Green Line* Standardaufgaben präsentieren zu können, und wünschen Ihnen und Ihren Schülern viel Erfolg und Freude bei der Arbeit mit *Green Line!*

Übersicht über die Aufgabentypen

Unit	Aufgabe	Aufgabentyp	offen	halboffen	geschlossen	Schwerpunkte
1	1a)–c)	Hörverstehen Detailverständnis			✔	Inhalt eines Gesprächs hörend erfassen
	2	Hör-/Sehverstehen Detailverständnis			✔	Inhalt eines Filmausschnitts verstehen
	3a), b)	Leseverstehen Detailverständnis/ Schreiben			✔	Inhalt eines Sachtextes lesend erfassen
	4	Schreiben	✔			die Fortsetzung einer Geschichte schreiben
	5	Sprechen	✔			anhand von Bildern über Australien sprechen
	6	Mediation		✔		wesentliche Informationen in der Muttersprache wiedergeben
	7	Grammatik			✔	notwendige und nicht-notwendige Relativsätze
	8	Grammatik			✔	*Relative clauses, contact clauses*
	9	Grammatik			✔	*let, make, have*
	10	Grammatik			✔	
	11	Grammatik		✔		*used to*
	12	Schreiben	✔			*How to: Explain a problem on the train*
	13	Lexik		✔		*odd one out*
	14	Lexik		✔		Wortschatz aus der *Unit: writing definitions*
	15	Lexik		✔		Wortschatz aus der *Unit*
	16	Lexik			✔	
	17	Lexik			✔	*Mixed bag*

2	1a), b)	Hörverstehen Detailverständnis			✔	Inhalt eines Gesprächs hörend erfassen
	2a), b)	Hör-/Sehverstehen Detailverständnis/ Schreiben		✔		Inhalt eines Filmausschnitts verstehen
	3a), b)	Leseverstehen Detailverständnis			✔	Inhalt von Stellenanzeigen lesend erfassen
	4	Schreiben	✔			eine Bewerbung schreiben
	5	Sprechen		✔		sich mit einem Partner über das Für und Wider zweier Berufspraktika unterhalten
	6	Mediation		✔		wesentliche Informationen in der Muttersprache wiedergeben
	7	Grammatik			✔	das Partizip anstelle eines Relativsatzes
	8	Grammatik			✔	adverbiale Nebensätze anstelle von Partizipialkonstruktionen
	9	Grammatik			✔	Partizipialkonstruktionen anstelle von adverbialen Nebensätzen
	10	Grammatik			✔	das Partizip und der Infinitiv nach Verben der Wahrnehmung und einem Objekt
	11	Grammatik			✔	*Revision:* die Wiedergabe der Zukunft
	12	Schreiben		✔		*How to: Talk about personal qualities*
	13	Lexik			✔	Wortbetonungen
	14	Lexik/Schreiben			✔	Wortfamilien
	15	Schreiben			✔	Berufe
	16	Lexik			✔	*Mixed bag*

Green Line 5
ISBN: 978-3-12-547164-1

Unit	Aufgabe	Aufgabentyp	offen	halboffen	geschlossen	Schwerpunkte
3	1a)	Hörverstehen Globalverständnis			✔	Inhalt einer *stage comedy* hörend erfassen
	1b)	Hörverstehen Detailverständnis			✔	
	2	Hör-/Sehverstehen Schreiben			✔	Inhalt eines Filmausschnitts verstehen
	3a), c)	Leseverstehen Detailverständnis			✔	Inhalt eines erzählenden Textes lesend erfassen
	3b)	Leseverstehen Globalverständnis			✔	
	4	Schreiben	✔			eine Geschichte fortsetzen / über Soaps schreiben / ein Drehbuchidee entwickeln
	5	Sprechen	✔			über die eigenen Gewohnheiten sprechen, Medien zu benutzen
	6	Mediation		✔		wesentliche Informationen in der Muttersprache wiedergeben
	7	Grammatik			✔	*Emphasis: Inversion*
	8	Grammatik			✔	*Emphasis*
	9	Grammatik			✔	*Simple and progressive forms*
	10	Grammatik			✔	*Revision:* Gegenwarts- und Vergangenheits-formen
	11	Lexik			✔	Wortschatz aus der *Unit*
	12	Lexik		✔		Wortschatz aus der *Unit: writing definitions*
	13	Lexik			✔	Partizipien als Adjektive
	14	Lexik			✔	Wortschatz aus der *Unit*
	15	Schreiben	✔			*How to: Argue politely*
	16a), b)	Lexik			✔	*Mixed bag*

4	1a)	Hörverstehen Globalverständnis			✔	Informationen aus einem Telefongespräch hörend erfassen
	1b)	Hör-/Sehverstehen Detailverständnis/ Schreiben		✔		
	2	Hör-/Sehverstehen Detailverständnis			✔	Inhalt eines Filmausschnitts verstehen
	3a), b)	Leseverstehen Detailverständnis			✔	Inhalt eines erzählenden Text lesend erfassen
	4	Schreiben	✔			einen Zeitungsartikel schreiben
	5	Sprechen	✔			über ein Foto zum Thema ‚Menschenrechte' sprechen
	6	Mediation		✔		wesentliche Informationen in der Fremdsprache wiedergeben
	7	Grammatik			✔	*Revision:* Präpositionen
	8	Grammatik			✔	*Revision: Gerund or infinitive*
	9	Grammatik			✔	
	10	Grammatik			✔	*Revision: Indirect speech*
	11	Grammatik			✔	*Revision: Modal auxiliaries and their substitutes*
	12	Schreiben	✔			*How to: Show everyday courage and support*
	13	Lexik			✔	Wortschatz aus der *Unit*
	14	Lexik			✔	Bedeutung und Verwendung von Verben
	15	Lexik			✔	*Mixed bag*

Green Line 5
ISBN: 978-3-12-547164-1

Unit 1 Australia

1 Listening: Australian crocodiles

a) *Listen to the dialogue. Then decide if the statements are right or wrong. Tick (✔) the correct box.*

	right	wrong
1. Speaker 1 is really excited about the outback because there are many exotic animals there.		✔
2. Most Australian animals scare tourists away.		
3. Dingoes can be really aggressive but they don't usually attack people.		
4. In the outback, more people die after allergic reactions to bee stings[1] than from spider bites.		
5. Saltwater crocodiles are more dangerous than sharks.		
6. The name of the saltwater crocodiles shows where they live.		
7. Crocodiles hide on river beds[2].		
8. Crocodiles do attack people every year.		

b) *Fill in the right word or phrase from the dialogue you have just heard.*

1. "Ha ha, OK Mr ____________. What do you want to tell me about now? I know that things don't happen like in the ____________ *Jaws* about the great ____________ shark."
2. "… about one ____________ dies from an attack from a great white shark."
3. "Sounds like ____________ to me."
4. "The saltwater crocodiles are actually ____________."
5. "Then we'll just ____________ in the fresh water."

c) *Listen again and tick (✔) the right answer.*

1. Aussies love telling tourists about …
   - A: harmless animals. ☐
   - B: dingoes. ☐
   - C: scary animals. ☐
   - D: aggressive people. ☐

2. On the northern coast of Australia there …
   - A: are dangerous animals in the water. ☐
   - B: are a lot of tourists. ☐
   - C: aren't any dingoes. ☐
   - D: are beautiful fish. ☐

3. To be safe in the outback you must …
   - A: stay in a group. ☐
   - B: stay away from rivers and still[3] waters. ☐
   - C: not sit in a boat. ☐
   - D: stay away from aggressive animals. ☐

4. More than two people in Australia …
   - A: die from crocodile attacks each year. ☐
   - B: are attacked by crocodiles but don't die. ☐
   - C: are killed by white sharks every year. ☐
   - D: don't go to the coast. ☐

[1]bee sting [ˈbiː stɪŋ] – *Bienenstich*, [2]river bed [ˌrɪvə ˈbed] – *Flussboden*, [3]still [stɪl] – *hier: stehend*

Green Line 5
ISBN: 978-3-12-547164-1

2 Understanding films: Choosing a career

Maya isn't sure which job she wants to do after school, so she's gone to a careers adviser who tells her about an interesting job …

Watch the film and put the sentence parts together. Draw lines.

1. For a hotel manager	to find out if a career is right for you.
2. Before you can be a hotel manager,	an office in Central London.
3. A work placement is a good way	a work placement in a hotel in Germany.
4. During a work placement you learn about	lots of different skills are important.
5. The careers adviser suggests	to arrive late for an interview.
6. She tells Maya to contact	you have to do a 3-year course.
7. Maya thinks that something was wrong	the positive and negative aspects of a job.
8. It doesn't make a good impression	with her outfit.

3 Reading: Movie reviews: *Australia*, 2008

☺

Take two unforgettable movies like *Gone With the Wind*[1] and *Out of Africa*[2], mix well (let Baz Luhrmann do the mixing), turn it on its head, and sit back and enjoy the wonderful film called simply *Australia*.

This story from the land 'down under' will turn your feelings inside out. Not only does director Luhrmann feature great actors (Nicole Kidman and Hugh Jackman), he also puts together great filming of the typical Australian outback with real historical events (the Stolen Generation and the Japanese attack of the city of Darwin). It's a story which is actually a mix of different stories. Nullah, a boy from the Stolen Generation, tells the story at the beginning. He explains what it is like to be caught between two worlds and the terrible way the Australian government dealt with the Aborigines.

Another storyline features Kidman's character Lady Sarah, one of the film's two main roles. She is an English lady who has to decide between taking the easy way out and selling her dead husband's ranch[3] or taking the hard way and saving it. Saving it, though, would mean Lady Sarah would have to learn to adapt to life in the wild outback. Jackman's character, the Drover

(because that's his job – driving cattle[4]), is the symbol for all that is difficult about the outback. These three stories give us a good look at Australian society, with all three 'ingredients[5]' of that society: the Aborigines (represented by Nullah), the British mother country (Lady Sarah) and the descendants[6] of the mother country (represented by Drover).

Add to this the love stories between Nullah and Sarah, who becomes like a mother to the boy, and between Sarah and Drover, who learn to respect each other's differences, and you've got an evening of beauty, surprise, feelings and entertainment. Australia will make you want to get there as soon as possible.

[1]Gone With the Wind [ˌɡɒn wɪð ðə 'wɪnd] – *Vom Winde verweht*, [2]Out of Africa [ˌaʊt‿əv‿'æfrɪkə] – *Jenseits von Afrika*, [3]ranch [rɑːntʃ] – *Farm*, [4]cattle ['kætl] – *Rind*, [5]ingredient [ɪn'ɡriːdɪənt] – *Zutat*, [6]descendant [dɪ'sendənt] – *Nachkomme*

Green Line 5
ISBN: 978-3-12-547164-1

☹

Baz Luhrmann, a native Australian, had a big dream when he began making a movie about his country. And the movie got very big – all 165 minutes of it (at least 45 minutes too long). It has thousands of cattle, aboriginal magic, important historical events, big-name stars in love (Nicole Kidman and Hugh Jackman) and of course the amazing landscape of the Australian outback. But while all of these things can make movies great, when Luhrmann puts them together it's just too much. There's no room left for a good story.
Luhrmann just lets us have a quick look at the historic problem of the "Stolen Generation" (part-Aboriginal children who were taken from their families and made to live in church orphanages[1]) through the character Nullah. As in any good mythical story, Nicole Kidman's character, Lady Sarah, becomes friends with and is like a mother to young Nullah. If there's a story in the movie then it is the one that involves Lady Sarah. She has come to Australia to see what her husband is doing on the cattle station but finds that he has been killed. She decides to save the cattle station and needs the help of the tough Drover (Jackman). At first these two characters, who are from very different worlds, hate each other. But as they are forced to work together to save the ranch they, of course, fall in love.
This typical, opposites-attract love story is so predictable that it almost makes you forget how beautiful the landscape is. If setting is important to you and you want to see some great Australian scenery[2] and hear some good Aboriginal music, go and see Australia. If you want a good plot that will hold your interest, stay home and read a good book instead.

[1]orphanage ['ɔːfnɪdʒ] – *Waisenhaus*, [2]scenery ['siːnəri] – landscape

a) *Read the two reviews about the film 'Australia'. Then tick (✔) the correct box.*

	right	wrong	not in the text
1. The first author mentions three unforgettable movies.		✔	
2. Mixing two great films and turning the result on its head, can become a great film, called *Australia*.			
3. Real historical events are mixed with great filming of the typical Australian outback.			
4. Nullah is an Aborigine.			
5. Nullah tells us what it is like to be caught between two worlds.			
6. The second part of the story is told by Lady Sarah.			
7. Lady Sarah decides to sell her dead husband's ranch.			
8. There are two love stories in the film, one between Nullah and Sarah, the other one between Sarah and Drover.			
9. Luhrmann puts so many things into his movie that it becomes just great.			
10. Lady Sarah has two children.			
11. Sarah and Drover are from two different worlds but after a while, they fall in love.			
12. The love story is unusual because it is of the opposites-attract type.			

Green Line 5
ISBN: 978-3-12-547164-1

b) *Answer the questions in no more than six words.*

1. What is Baz Luhrmann's role in the film?

   He's the director.

2. What real events are featured in the film? Name one.

3. How did Drover get his name?

4. How many storylines are there in the film?

5. Where was Baz Luhrmann born?

6. According to the second text, what is missing in the film?

7. What does Lady Sarah find out when she comes to Australia?

8. How do Lady Sarah and Drover first feel about each other?

9. What kind of love story is in the film?

10. What can you do instead of watching the film?

4 Writing: Better safe than sorry

Read the text and continue the story.
Write it in your exercise book.

TIP
1. Find the important story elements that are introduced at the beginning of the text below.
2. Go through every story element and write down how you could continue each of them.

When I was walking down Bangalay Drive in Port Macquarie one afternoon last summer, I was very excited because I was looking forward to going to the beautiful lighthouse and lovely sandy beach with my cousin Milly. I was on holiday on the east coast of Australia for the first time and my ideas were centred on adventure!
Suddenly I heard a hissing[1] noise very close to me. Although I looked around immediately, I couldn't see anything. I knew my cousin was eager for me to arrive so that we could go and have fun, so, like any nice girl who wants to be on time, I decided to ignore the noise and continue my walk to Milly's house.
Today I know that I should have been much more careful! I could have avoided[2] great danger if I had not just looked around but also checked my handbag. "Better safe than sorry[3]" should have been my motto. Well, I just didn't think about it at the time and I was new to Australia. …

[1]hissing [ˈhɪsɪŋ] – *zischend,* [2]to avoid [əˈvɔɪd] – *vermeiden,* [3]Better safe than sorry – it is better to be careful than to risk danger

Green Line 5
ISBN: 978-3-12-547164-1

5 Speaking: About Australia

Prepare a short talk (2 minutes) on Australia. Look at the pictures for help and try to include everything you know.

6 Mediation: Salties

Situation: Your little brother has asked you for help. He has to do a school project "Reiseempfehlungen für Australien-Touristen". He has to warn tourists about saltwater[1] crocodiles. On the Internet you find this article:

The saltwater crocodile is the world's largest crocodile. You find saltwater crocodiles around the coast of Australia anywhere north of the Southern Tropics and inland for 100 km or more.
In the early 1970s their number had fallen to about 5,000 and they stopped hunting them. Today there are about 85,000 in the Northern Territory alone, with tens of thousands more in Queensland and Western Australia.

The following information is to warn people of the dangers that may arise if you meet these creatures. Many people have died over the years because they did not take the warning signs seriously.
Crocodiles are a danger at any time, but they are even more dangerous at night. Don't forget that they are most active at night and be very careful after dark. Another piece of advice you should follow is to avoid places where animals or cattle drink. That's where crocodiles usually wait for a chance to attack.
Most important if camping, always keep the camp clean! You should not leave any food or rubbish outside. The smell might invite hungry crocodiles.

Finally, don't panic when you spot one. A crocodile that you can see is not as dangerous as one that you can't see. But never ever dare to provoke it!

No warning signs – no crocodiles?

DO NOT SWIM no matter how hot it may be or how inviting the water may be. Remember, just because you don't see a crocodile doesn't mean it's not there!

[1]saltwater ['sɔːlt,wɔːtə] – *Salzwasser*

Green Line 5
ISBN: 978-3-12-547164-1

For your brother, write down in German …

1. … in which areas of Australia the Salties live.

2. … which dangerous situations tourists should avoid.

Green Line 5
ISBN: 978-3-12-547164-1

7 Gracey and Angela

***Which, who, whose** or contact clause? Put in commas where you need them.*

Gracey is a part-Aboriginal girl ______________ thinks she is being colonized by her friend Angela. Angela however ______________ feels that she has always been caring about Gracey is shocked by her friend's ideas. One day the two meet at a mall for a rally ______________ people have organized to support the Aborigines. Angela ______________ idea it has been to support Gracey at the rally thinks of herself as Gracey's best friend. The moment in ______________ she realizes how much Gracey dislikes her help makes Angela angry and sad. In Angela's eyes it's all a big misunderstanding ______________ she would like to talk to Gracey about. The atmosphere ______________ is a bit cool quickly changes to cold and aggressive. The argument at the jewellery store ______________ Angela goes to to pick up her mother's watch becomes the turning point of the story.

8 The Great Barrier Reef

Link the sentences by using relative or contact clauses.

1. The Great Barrier Reef is one of the natural wonders of the world. It begins just off the coast of Bundaberg and extends[1] over 2,000 km north to western Papua New Guinea.

   ____

   ____

2. It is in fact not a single reef, but a collection of over 2,900 individual reefs, 300 coral cays and 600 continental islands. It is full of life, colour and adventure.

   ____

   ____

3. The Great Barrier Reef Marine Park was opened in 1975. It covers[2] over 98% of the area.

   ____

4. There are damaged corals at the Great Barrier Reef. Here you can see an example of one.

   ____

5. The green season starts with the first of the monsoon[3] rains in November and ends in May. It provides[4] 75–90% of the region's rainfall.

   ____

   ____

[1]to extend [ɪk'stend] – *sich erstrecken,* [2]to cover ['kʌvə] – *bedecken,* [3]monsoon [mɒn'su:n] – *Monsun,* [4]to provide [prə'vaɪd] – *liefern*

Green Line 5
ISBN: 978-3-12-547164-1

9 The next day

George had a party yesterday. Now he is talking to his friend Luke on the phone.

*Put in the correct forms of **let, make** or **have**.*

(…) "Yeah, it's been a terrible day! Dad says he'll never __________ me have a party here again."

(…) "Well, it was pretty mad! He wanted to __________ the mess cleaned up as soon as you'd all gone. But I was so dead tired that Mum __________ me go to bed. But they didn't __________ me sleep long." (…) "The house looked awful! My brother wanted to help, but Dad wouldn't __________ him do anything – he __________ me do it all by myself, apart from the broken window – we'll have to __________ it repaired. And Dad is going to __________ me pay for it!"

(…) "Yeah. Someone had even been sick in the hall, and Dad __________ me start with that."

(…) "When I said that we should __________ it done professionally, Dad got really angry."

(…) "No, sorry, I can't. Dad is __________ me stay in every night this week." (…) "Thanks! OK, bye!"

10 Situations

*Look at the pictures and say what is happening. Form sentences with **let, make** or **have**.*

1 Peter – his car – repair

2 Her friend – her hair – cut

3 The Smiths – milk – deliver

4 His parents – Steve – go on a school exchange to Australia

5 Dean's dad – the teenagers – listen to him

6 Milly – Daisy – play with her teddy bear

1. Peter is having his car repaired.
2. ______________________________
3. ______________________________
4. ______________________________
5. ______________________________
6. ______________________________

Green Line 5
ISBN: 978-3-12-547164-1

11 Life back then from 1901 to 1914

This is part of an account of life in Australia from 1901 to 1914 in the eyes of a working-class man.

Change the account by using forms of ***used to, didn't use to*** *or questions with* ***did … use to?*** *where you think they make sense.*

1. "Life back then was really hard. I had to work under bad conditions and the work itself was dangerous. People were afraid for their health. I earned just A$5.50 and for that I had to work a 50-hour week!"

2. "Today I'm often asked: 'Did you really work that hard? Did you have to work so many hours?'"

3. "Today's young people just can't believe it. You see, it wasn't like today. We worked like dogs to put food on the table. Nowadays life is easier for workers but it wouldn't be if we hadn't fought for it in earlier times. We pushed for higher pay and better working conditions."

4. "My house was quite small and as we worked all day, we had little time for leisure activities."

5. "Australia had six separate colonies, but in 1901 the colonies became one nation. It was then governed by just one Federation. We became the Commonwealth of Australia."

6. "We celebrated the Federation across the nation and had a good time. We weren't a multicultural society back then. The population was mainly people directly from the British Isles or Australian-born white lads. A lot of people saw Britain as their home and education was influenced by British beliefs."

Green Line 5
ISBN: 978-3-12-547164-1

12 How to: Explain a problem on the train

Imagine you are on holiday in Australia. On the train your rucksack gets stolen. You have all your money and papers in it. The man sitting next to you wants to help you.

Make a dialogue with the help of the useful phrases or with your own words.

USEFUL PHRASES

help? • rucksack with all my money in it was stolen • describe what happened? • notice anything? • use your mobile phone? • number of the German consulate? • police officer on this train • your passport? • fill out these forms so that I can help you • German consulate can give you a new passport for your flight home

Start like this:

Man: May I help you?

You: ______

Man: ______

You: ______

Man: ______

You: ______

Man: ______

You: ______

Police officer: ______

You: ______

Police officer: ______

13 Find the odd one out

... and say why you think it is odd.

1. shark • box jellyfish • koala • crocodile

______

2. prison •promise • perspective • princess

______

3. Aboriginal • Asian • British • Australian

______

4. ancestor • convict • criminal • prisoner

______

Green Line 5
ISBN: 978-3-12-547164-1

14 Word power

Write definitions for the following expressions.

1. Asian-Pacific: ______________________________
2. outback: ______________________________
3. penal colony: ______________________________
4. foreign: ______________________________
5. survey: ______________________________
6. Aussie: ______________________________
7. racist: ______________________________

15 Find the right words

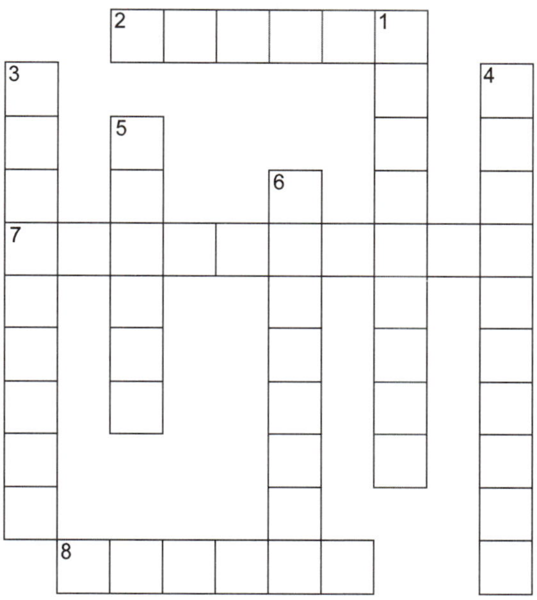

Down: ↓

1. someone who is always worrying about everything
3. a form of government ruled by the people and not by a king or queen
4. Australia's black inhabitants
5. something from a distant and foreign country, e. g. a fruit like a coconut
6. an animal that only exists in Australia

Across: →

2. if you ask someone to give you something for a special time
7. around the earth, there is a natural protection from the sun, but it has a huge hole over Australia
8. an area with lots of trees

16 Fill in the right words

Many young visitors get ______________ by the idea that Australia used to be a ______________ colony. The British really sent shiploads of ______________ to Oz and __________ thousands of ______________ spend the rest of their lives there. They ____________ them do a lot of the __________ work like building roads. Although there really were some ______________ criminals, judges in Britain also __________ people sent to Australia simply for ______________ apples. While most immigrants __________ _____ come from Europe, now they almost all come from __________. The role of Australia in the __________-____________ world is important.

Green Line 5
ISBN: 978-3-12-547164-1

Favourite leisure __________ are having barbies or __________ on the ocean waves. Tourists are offered adventure trips in the __________ or to Uluru. The Australian coast is __________ to be fairly dangerous, and so are rivers because of their __________ population. Red-back spiders are __________ to be the most dangerous __________ in Australia, much more dangerous than the great white __________.

17 Mixed bag: The Stolen Generation

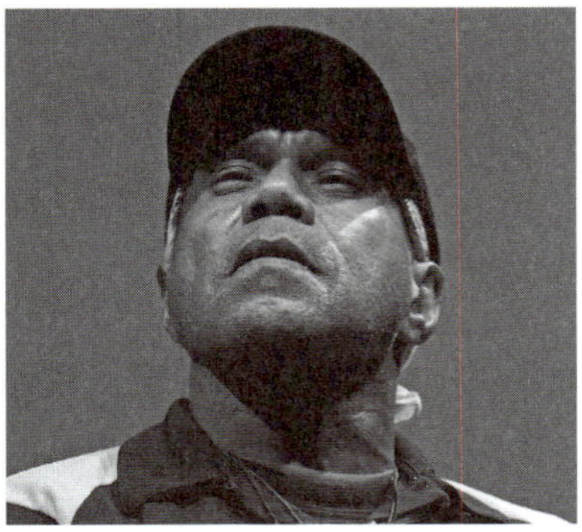

Fill in the missing words.

This is the story of Archie Roach, a 45-year-old part-Aborigine, __________ belongs[1] to Australia's 'Stolen Generation'. Three-year-old Archie, __________ lived in Framlingham in southeastern Australia, was taken from his mom, __________ was told that he was being escorted to a picnic by some officers. His aunt, __________ tried to scare[2] those officers with a gun, had to give __________ because the gun was __________ loaded. Later Archie was told that his family had died __________ a fire. The people __________ looked after him in an orphanage tried to __________ him into a 'white' __________ by making his curly hair straight. The idea was __________ part-Aborigine children had __________ __________ 'civilized' by adopting[3] __________ into white society. The reason __________ Archie __________ taken was that his grandfather had __________ white. At the age of 14 Archie learned that __________ mother had still been alive until recently and he understood __________ he had __________ lied to his whole life. He then __________ away from his wrong 'home' and spent the __________ 14 years drinking, sleeping __________ parks and __________ the guitar to have enough money __________ the next bottle. Yet Archie's story took a __________ turn: He began writing and singing __________. His song Took the Children Away became a real hit in 1987.

[1]to belong [bɪˈlɒŋ] – *gehören*, [2]to scare sb [skeə] – *jmdm. Angst einjagen*, [3]to adopt [əˈdɒpt] – *adoptieren*

Green Line 5
ISBN: 978-3-12-547164-1

Unit 2 What next?

1 Listening: Careers talk

Listen to a teacher and his students.

a) *Right or wrong? Tick (✔).*

	right	wrong
1. The teacher says it isn't easy for actors to find work.	✔	
2. Peter doesn't believe that teachers are badly paid.		
3. Students' interests and hobbies are not so important when it comes to choosing a career.		
4. The teacher asks the students to write one list of jobs they would like and another list of jobs they would hate.		
5. He tells the students that watching TV can never lead to a career.		
6. Peter wants to give his teacher the impression that he has lots of talents.		
7. The teacher says everyone must take part in a computer programme to find the right career.		
8. He admits that he doesn't know about all the careers which exist.		

b) *Which of these careers did you hear about? Tick (✔) the right boxes.*

1 ☐

2 ☐

3 ☐

4 ☐

5 ☐

6 ☐

7 ☐

8 ☐

Green Line 5
ISBN: 978-3-12-547164-1

2 Understanding films: Applying for a job

Maya has her first job interview and is very nervous.

Watch the film and do the tasks.

a) *What does Maya say about the working conditions in a hotel? Collect three points.*

1. ______________________________

2. ______________________________

3. ______________________________

b) *Complete the sentences with the right information from the film.*

1. Maya would like to do a course in ______________________________
2. After that she'd like to apply for a job as ______________________________
3. Mr McFarlane tells Maya that she would start ______________________________
4. Work placements in this company normally last ______________________________
5. Mr McFarlane isn't happy to hear that Maya isn't always on time and she's afraid that she's lost the chance of ______________________________
6. Maya is very happy when she hears that she'll be sent to ______________________________

3 Reading: Job advertisements on the Internet

Live-in au pair needed in Ireland Live-in position available in Ireland, looking after one child age 7, starting January 2010 for up to 12 months (possibly more), own bedroom and bathroom, TV, DVD player, laptop, radio etc. Must be kind, fun, reliable[1]. Must have references. For more information e-mail hlkennedy@testireland.net	**Ad Posting Job Earn up to $ 50,000 per month** Are you interested in working part-time from home for some extra money? Or are you looking for a full-time career making $ 50,000 per month? For more information visit: www.rcbd.biz or email to info@rcbd.biz or call 456-432-3338
Student Adviser Do you love education? Join America's largest Online University and make a difference in the lives of others! Advise working adults about applying for college. Offer students across the country the highest level of one-on-one customer service and support. For this position you need confidence, strong organizational and communication skills, you must be a guide for others and be dedicated[2] to the job. You must have good knowledge of business, education, have technology adviser skills as well as very good presentation skills in front of both large and small groups. A university education is preferred. PhoenixUOnline@u-phoenix.edu	**Store Manager** El Taco LLC offers excellent career opportunities. We are looking for people who want to build a career in the restaurant business. As a Store Manager you will be organizing a restaurant team that delivers the highest results in the areas of quality, guest service, sales, cleanliness[3] and food preparation and presentation. You will also be hiring, training and managing your own staff. You'll communicate with your Area Director/Area Manager about business goals[4] – how to improve the restaurant. If you feel you are the right person for the job, send your resume/CV today. eltaco_info@eltaco.com

Green Line 5
ISBN: 978-3-12-547164-1

Graphic Designer/3D Animator[5] with Games Industry Experience	Doctor's office in Pasadena has a full-time opening for an experienced Receptionist/ Medical Assistant[8].
Large software company in The Eastside, WA area needs a graphic designer/3D Animator. This great opportunity pays $28+/hr depending on[6] experience. You will design the "look and feel" of software, web sites and print media. Qualifications: **Must have game industry, 3D animator experience** Strong communication skills are necessary[7] and you must be able to meet deadlines in a fast-moving industry. Must notice detail and be able to work as a team player. University: Design, Graphic Design, Fine Arts, Industrial Design … Contact: eastsidedesign@web.net	Areas of responsibility include patient check-in and check-out, answering phones, preparing forms for patient visits, general medical assistant duties. Applicants should have a high school diploma, have at leasta six months' receptionist and/or medical assistant experience; excellent telephone skills would be helpful good people, communication and computer skills necessary; knowledge of insurance[9] and accounting helpful. Job is full time, Monday through Friday. Send your resume/CV: dr_cook@pasadena.net

[1]reliable [rɪ'laɪəbl] – who you can trust, [2]dedicated ['dedɪkeɪtɪd] – who loves the job, [3]cleanliness ['klenlɪnɪs] – *Sauberkeit*, [4]goal [gəʊl] – *Ziel*, [5]animator ['ænɪmeɪtə] – *Trickfilmzeichner*, [6]to depend on [dɪ'pend‿ɒn] – *abhängen von*, [7]necessary ['nesəsri] – what you need to have, [8]medical assistant [ˌmedɪkl ə'sɪstnt] – *Arzthelfer/in*, [9]insurance [ɪn'ʃʊərns] – *Versicherung*

a) *Tick (✔) the right answer.*

1. The au pair in Ireland will have to …
   - A: drive the family car. ☐
   - B: share a bathroom. ☐
   - C: help as well as entertain a child. ☐

2. The ad posting job is perfect if you …
   - A: have a university education. ☐
   - B: want to work in a team with others. ☐
   - C: have to look after small children at home. ☐

3. The student adviser must be good at …
   - A: teaching groups of students. ☐
   - B: giving talks in front of an audience. ☐
   - C: dealing with personal problems. ☐

4. The student adviser will give advice …
   - A: in the students' homes. ☐
   - B: online. ☐
   - C: in an office at Phoenix University. ☐

5. The store manager will not be involved in …
   - A: choosing new cooks and waiters. ☐
   - B: deciding what the different dishes cost. ☐
   - C: building the restaurant. ☐

6. The graphic designer should be someone who …
   - A: has done this kind of work before. ☐
   - B: wants to learn about design on the job. ☐
   - C: prefers to work independently. ☐

7. The graphic designer will earn more than $28 if he/she …
   - A: has a university degree. ☐
   - B: is a team player. ☐
   - C: has a lot of experience. ☐

8. The doctor hopes the new receptionist will …
   - A: be able to deal with office paperwork. ☐
   - B: have worked in a hospital for six months. ☐
   - C: visit patients' homes with him/her. ☐

Green Line 5
ISBN: 978-3-12-547164-1

b) *Which of the ads mention these qualifications or abilities (Fähigkeiten)? Write down the names of the jobs.*

1. Formal education ________ student adviser, ________
2. Practical experience in the same kind of job ________
3. Computer skills ________
4. Working together with other people employed there ________

4 Writing: A letter of application

Imagine you are someone who wants to apply for one of the jobs in Ex. 3. Plan and write your letter of application.

a) *Choose a job and make notes for your letter.*

Why I am writing this letter ________

My qualifications and experience ________

Why I would be the right person ________

Friendly, hopeful ending ________

What I am enclosing ________ CV, ________

b) *Now write the letter in your exercise book. Remember what your have learned about the form and style of such letters.*

address	own address
Application	date
Dear Madam or Sir,	
…	
Yours sincerely	
…	

Green Line 5
ISBN: 978-3-12-547164-1

5 Speaking: Work experience

You and your partner are going to do work experience next week. One of you is going to look after animals in a zoo and the other will be working for a firm which develops software for other firms.

Discuss the advantages of your job and the disadvantages of your partner's.
Prepare the roles using the notes and your own ideas.

(A) Job at a zoo

pros	cons
– work with animals and people	– often start work early
– fresh air	– get dirty
– different every day	– dangerous
– want to be vet	– outside in bad weather
–	–
–	–
–	–

(B) Job at software firm

pros	cons
– work with computers	– work alone
– use own ideas	– same work every day
– work office hours	– unhealthy, sit still
– many job opportunities later	– work with business people
–	–
–	–
–	–

6 Mediation: Pupils' reports

Situation: Your e-mail partner in Scotland has sent you her school's online magazine with pupils' reports about their work experience placements.

For my work experience placement I went to Grafton Hospital. I settled down quickly and felt great because everyone was so kind. My favourite thing during my placement was being allowed to observe[1] an operation. This was quite fascinating as it was my first real-life opportunity to watch an operation. I also assisted doctors dealing with minor accidents (cuts and burns), and I found this very rewarding[2], knowing that I had been able to help the patients. Almost every day I did some paperwork and work at the computer. Even though the office work did get a bit boring at times, I had a good time with the staff[3] there. I was also interested in the work of nurses and helped a nurse with diagnostic tests. I learned so many new things and met some impressive people. I can definitely see myself going into the field of medicine.

Catherine Wade

For my work experience I went to Longwood Primary School. As soon as I arrived at the school I felt really welcome. Working with the children was very enjoyable. The best part for me was the storytelling. They made up their own stories, and I was amazed at how creative they were. As I am not a very patient person, though, I would say that working with very young children is not a job for me. As much as I loved the children, I think my work experience has helped me to see this. All the teachers and staff were very supportive and answered any questions I had. At the end of my time there I received[4] a good report and was happy with my performance. Maybe in the future I will consider teaching older children.

Rachel McGowan

[1]to observe [əb'zɜ:v] – to watch, [2]rewarding [rɪ'wɔ:dɪŋ] – which gives you a good feeling, [3]staff [stɑ:f] – the people who work there, [4]to receive [rɪ'si:v] – to get

Green Line 5
ISBN: 978-3-12-547164-1

As your class is going to take part in work experience placements, too, you bring the reports to school. Your teacher asks you to tell your class about the experiences the English pupils have had. These are the questions he asks:

1. Wo haben die beiden Mädchen gearbeitet?

2. Was empfand Catherine als positiv?

3. Was fand Catherine nicht so spannend?

4. Was war Catherines beste Erfahrung?

5. Würde Catherine den Beruf später ausüben wollen?

6. Und Rachel? Was hat ihr bei ihrer Arbeit besonders gefallen?

7. Was hat Rachel bei der Arbeit herausgefunden?

8. Würde Rachel den Beruf später ausüben wollen?

9. Waren die Arbeitgeber zufrieden? Schreiben die Mädchen etwas darüber?

Green Line 5
ISBN: 978-3-12-547164-1

7 Relative clauses and participles

Rewrite the sentences using participles in the present or past tense.

1. Students who want to become engineers often choose a work experience placement in a factory.

____

2. Some big firms have special programmes that have been planned to help student visitors.

____

3. Read what one of the young people who is doing work experience has written in her report.

____

4. "Most of the work that is done by the engineers is too difficult for me."

____

5. "But I'm sure the experiences which have been offered to me here will be very useful in future."

____

8 An exciting evening at work

Read this newspaper report about Ryan.

Having had a weekend job in a garage, Ryan wanted a different kind of holiday job. He found work at a restaurant known to be very expensive. One evening, having been asked to help one of the waitresses, Ryan was clearing a table. Then he heard sounds coming from the table in the corner. Turning round, he saw two men exchanging money and small packets[1]. Shocked by what he had seen, he informed the manager. Arriving at the restaurant ten minutes later, the police found more money and drugs hidden in the men's shoes.

What did Ryan tell his friends in direct speech? Turn the (underlined) participle constructions into new sentences.

"After I had had a weekend job in a garage, I wanted

____

____

____

____

____

____

____

[1]small packets [smɔːl ˈpækɪts] – *Päckchen*

Green Line 5
ISBN: 978-3-12-547164-1

9 A career as a journalist

Rewrite the text using participles in place of the underlined phrases.

Nicole wants to become a journalist because she has often worked on the school magazine. She enjoys writing texts which inform students and parents about interesting events, and she once reported about plans for new school rules that were heavily criticised by students. Nicole knows that when she tries to get a job with a newspaper, she must have some experience or qualifications which make her a suitable person for the job. She often sends short articles to magazines. She hopes that they will be published[1]. After she has left school, Nicole plans to take a creative writing course which is advertised on all the career websites.

Nicole wants to become a journalist, having often worked on

[1]to publish [ˈpʌblɪʃ] – *veröffentlichen*

10 What did Gavin see and hear?

Yesterday Gavin had to pick up rubbish in the park. But he didn't find it so boring.

Use these verbs and the present participle.

hear • listen to • notice • see • watch

fight drive play talk sit

1. He watched some children
2.
3.
4.
5.

Green Line 5
ISBN: 978-3-12-547164-1

11 Talking about the future

Complete the dialogue with the right form of the future.

Luke: When I leave school I ______________________ (be) a tennis trainer.

Jane: I don't think anyone ______________________ (give) you a job as a trainer. You aren't patient enough.

Luke: Maybe you're right. But sport ______________________ (always/be) my favourite hobby.

Jane: Mine, too. I ______________________ (start) playing badminton next month.

Luke: Badminton? That's not as good as tennis. I ______________________ (play) in a match tomorrow afternoon. Why don't you come and watch?

Jane: Sorry, I ______________________ (meet) my cousin from Bristol at the station. Her train ______________ (arrive) at 3.20.

Luke: Bring her along, too. I ______________________ (win) this match!

Jane: I ______________________ (think) about it.

12 How to: Talk about personal qualities

Imagine you are being interviewed for a work experience placement in a TV producer's office. Answer the interviewer's questions. (Remember – you want this job!)

Interviewer: How would you describe yourself?

You: ______________________

____

Interviewer: What are you especially good at?

You: ______________________

____

Interviewer: Are there any kinds of work you don't like?

You: ______________________

____

Interviewer: Why do you think you would be good at this job?

You: ______________________

____

Green Line 5
ISBN: 978-3-12-547164-1

13 Which part of the word is stressed?

Put the words into the right group.

~~applicant~~ • appointment • architect • construction • creative • engineer • guarantee • hairdresser • musician • questionnaire • signature • sincerely • suitable

● • •	• ● •	• • ●
applicant		

14 Word families

Look at the underlined words. Complete the sentences with a word from the same word family.

1. Mrs Lawson <u>employs</u> 37 people, and they all say she is a good ________________.
2. Hundreds of people have <u>applied</u> for the job, but only 20 ________________ are going to be invited for interviews.
3. Mike was asked to <u>sign</u> the form, but he didn't want to put his ________________ on something he hadn't read.
4. Lenny has decided to do <u>social</u> work because he wants to help the poor in our ________________.
5. Emily can't <u>imagine</u> working as a police officer. – But she isn't a very ________________ person.

15 Different jobs

What jobs are these people talking about?

1. "… can be dangerous when a whole factory is burning, but it's exciting too …" ________________
2. "… enjoy solving technical problems – bridges, tunnels …" ________________
3. "… do interviews when we're looking for people to work for our company …" ________________
4. "… but I don't go round catching thieves and drug dealers all day." ________________
5. "… designing and making plans for all kinds of buildings …" ________________
6. "… I can usually tell you whether it's going to rain next weekend or not …" ________________

Green Line 5
ISBN: 978-3-12-547164-1

16 Mixed bag: Linda can't decide

Fill in the missing words. Choose them from the list below the text.

Linda is finding it difficult to decide (a) __________ a career. She (b) ______________ her work experience at a hotel, but that kind of work didn't really (c) ______________ her. She enjoyed (d) ________________ to the international guests because she is (e) ________________ in three languages, but she found the office work boring. "I did think about becoming a (f) ______________________," she says, "but I would have to (g) ________________ so many exams. I like the idea of working with people, (h) ___________________ families, so (i) ________________________ I've been finding out about social workers. They don't earn much at first, but their pay (j) _______________ when they (k) _______________ higher qualifications."

(l) ___________ the way, next week Linda is starting a holiday job at a campsite, where she is (m) _______________ to work for lots of families. Will this work experience help her to choose (n) __________ right career?

a)	for	on	over	h) most	mainly	much
b)	made	applied	had	i) recent	lastly	recently
c)	like	suit	pass	j) rises	raises	rose
d)	talking	talk	helping	k) are	become	get
e)	fluent	flying	well	l) By	On	In
f)	legal	lawyer	law	m) like	likely	possible
g)	make	part	pass	n) a	the	her

Green Line 5
ISBN: 978-3-12-547164-1

Unit 3 Media-mad

1 Listening: Modern comedy

a) *Listen to a comedian on stage. Then look at the pictures. In each line of pictures (1–4) tick (✔) the right one.*

1. A:  ☐ B:  ☐ C:  ☐

2. A:  ☐ B:  ☐ C:  ☐

3. A:  ☐ B:  ☐ C:  ☐

4. A:  ☐ B:  ☐ C:  ☐

b) *Tick (✔) the right answer.*

1. The girls on the bus are …
   - A: popular and well-liked. ☐
   - B: polite and well-liked. ☐
   - C: beautiful and well-liked. ☐

2. Last weekend the girls have made …
   - A: more than three friends. ☐
   - B: more than eight friends. ☐
   - C: more than 14 friends. ☐

3. The comedian …
   - A: often meets new people. ☐
   - B: does not want to meet new people. ☐
   - C: does not really meet new people. ☐

4. One of the girls …
   - A: counts her friends. ☐
   - B: calls her friends. ☐
   - C: writes texts to her friends. ☐

5. The comedian …
   - A: wonders how many friends the girls have. ☐
   - B: wants to have 100 friends, too. ☐
   - C: wants to invite 100 friends to his birthday party. ☐

6. On the bus, the girls are …
   - A: listening to music on their cell phones. ☐
   - B: playing with their cell phones. ☐
   - C: talking to friends on their cell phones. ☐

7. The comedian …
   - A: has left his cell phone at home. ☐
   - B: has left his cell phone in the car. ☐
   - C: has his cell phone with him. ☐

8. The comedian …
   - A: knows the girls' names. ☐
   - B: knows all his friends by name. ☐
   - C: does not know his friends' names. ☐

Green Line 5
ISBN: 978-3-12-547164-1

2 Understanding films: Starting a new job

Watch the film and tick (✔) the right sentences. Sometimes more than one answer is correct.

1. ☐ Maya looks disappointed when she enters the hotel.
   ☐ Maya says hello in German.
   ☐ She wants to see the hotel manager.
   ☐ She wants to see the head of reception[1].

2. ☐ Her Name is Nicole Schuster.
   ☐ Her name is Nicole Schmidt.
   ☐ She speaks English well.
   ☐ She tells Maya to improve her German skills.

3. ☐ The caller wants a room for five nights from the 21st.
   ☐ The caller's last name is Xiao.
   ☐ The caller's last name is Cheng.
   ☐ He'd like a single smoker room.

[1]head of reception [ˌhed‿əv rɪˈsepʃn] – *Empfangschef/in*

3 Reading: The chance of her life

(1) "Hey, you! Yes, I mean you with the pink pullover, can you come over here?" Carolyn's heart jumped. They had finally noticed her.

(2) When she had arrived with her parents at the little village in the Highlands she had expected 20 days of being bored, of long walks to the ruins of castles and villages long forgotten – except[1] by her father, of course – and of endless evenings spent in their hotel room listening to him talking about Scottish history in general[2], and especially the role of their family. But then she had discovered the film team who were taking scenes for her favourite soap. And he was there, he, Hendrik Benson, the star of the soap, the hero. From then on Carolyn had hung around the film camp almost every day, any minute she could get away from her parents, always hoping that they – no, that *he* – would see her and ask her to join them.

(3) And now … Carolyn walked slowly towards the man who had called her.

"You're interested in what we're doing here, right? Do you know the production we're working on?" he asked.

"Sure, I haven't missed one episode so far," she replied.

"I thought so. You've been hanging around here for a few days, I thought you might be interested in working with us. Would you?"

"Uh … oh … yes, sure, but …"

"You'd have to ask your parents first, and they'll want to know who we are, what we're doing here, what you'll be doing here and so on, right?" the man laughed. "And I'm sure you'd like to know more about the work, too.'

"Well, yes, of course. Will I see Hendrik Benson?" Caroly asked quickly.

"Sure you will, if things go well. I suggest you go to your parents and ask them. They can come over here and talk to me if they want to. Give them my card". He took a card out of his pocket and gave it to Carolyn.

(4) Carolyn took the card and hurried home to the hotel. On the way she thought of what her role would be : she might have a bad accident and Hendrik would save her/she might fall into a lake and Hendrik would save her/she might get lost in the mountains (there were enough lakes to fall into or mountains to get lost in) …

(5) At the hotel her father was quite strict about the whole thing.

Green Line 5
ISBN: 978-3-12-547164-1

"We haven't come all this way just to see our daughter spend her time with some silly film team while mum and I do the sightseeing tours alone", he said. "We know about our family history. You should learn about it, my dear." "Adam, let's at least talk to the man", her mum answered. "Your sightseeing tours aren't Carolyn's idea of a holiday. You've noticed that, haven't you?"
Finally her father agreed.

(6) So Carolyn and her mum went to the film camp. The man – Robert S. Halmond, Executive Producer[3], his card said – told her mum that for some scenes they needed extras, that they needed hands for all kinds of jobs like making coffee and so on, and that Carolyn would work for about six hours a day, four days in all, including[4] two nights when shots had to be taken in the dark. She would get some money, not much but at least more than a week's pocket money.

[1]except [ɪk'sept] – *außer,* [2]in general [ɪn‿'dʒenrəl] – *im Allgemeinen,* [3]Executive Producer [ɪgˌzekjʊtɪv prə'dju:sə] – *Produzent,* [4]including [ɪn'klu:dɪŋ] – *einschließlich*

a) *Read the text and the sentences. Put each sentence at the end of one paragraph. Write the numbers in the boxes.*

- ☐ A "But I won't go to those people, you can make sure that our daughter doesn't get in trouble."
- ☐ B "That way your parents will know that this is a serious offer, OK?"
- ☐ C She had even tried to talk to the men who were guarding the area but they had only smiled.
- ☐ D That would save her holidays.
- ☐ E And she could start at once, right now.
- ☐ F And Hendrik would save her.

b) *Which heading matches which paragraph? Write the numbers in the boxes.*

- ☐ Dreaming
- ☐ The situation changes
- ☐ Talking business
- ☐ The offer
- ☐ Yes!
- ☐ Different opinions about holidays

c) *Tick (✔) the correct boxes.*

Who ...	Carolyn	Hendrik Benson	Robert S. Halmond
1. is on holiday in the Scottish Highlands?			
2. is the star of the soap?			
3. makes Carolyn a serious offer?			
4. might save Carolyn in a film scene?			
5. has talked to Carolyn?			
6. is not interested in sightseeing?			
7. is the producer of the soap?			
8. would do all kinds of jobs for the film team?			

Green Line 5
ISBN: 978-3-12-547164-1

4 Writing: Soaps!

Choose one of the exercises. Write about 120 words.

1. *Write an ending to Carolyn's story. Think about the following questions:*
   Will she talk to Hendrik Benson? Will the job be as interesting as she thinks?

OR

2. *Write about your favourite TV program/soap. What is so exciting about it that you watch it (almost) every day?*

OR

3. *You may have watched a lot of movies at the cinema or on TV. Develop and write down the outline of a screenplay in which you would like to be the hero.*

5 Speaking: My use of media

Prepare a short talk (2–3 minutes) for the class about your personal use of media. The following points should be mentioned:

1. What kind of media do you use? (telephone / mobile, Internet, television, radio, MP3, books, newspapers, magazines …)
2. Which of these is the most important to you / the one that you use most often?
3. What do you use them for? (talking to friends, getting information, playing games, listening to music, being entertained …)
4. How much time do you spend using them every day?
5. Do you think you should spend less time with media?
6. Do you sometimes run out of time for other things (homework, sports, meeting people) because you play around with media?

Make notes first.

Green Line 5
ISBN: 978-3-12-547164-1

6 Mediation: An interview

Situation: From a trip, your dad brought a British teen magazine (Mag) for you. You read an interview with Emma Short (ES), a successful commercial director.

Mag: When did you realize that you wanted to become a film director?
ES: I've loved films and videos ever since I was about twelve years old. When I asked the school careers adviser about it at the age of 14, he didn't take me very seriously. When I was 15, I was given a second-hand camera. That was great – at last I could make my own short films.
Mag: Are your parents in the film business?
ES: Oh, no, not at all. My dad is a social worker and my mum is a teacher. She's Chinese, you know.
Mag: What did you do after you left school?
ES: I did a film course at the University of Westminster. We made a lot of short films and videos but of course, it wasn't all fun. University courses never are!
Mag: What is your work exactly?
ES: Well, before you make a film there are meetings with the advertising agency. Everything is planned and the script has to be written, so that the agency knows what the film will be like when it's finished. Then when you make the film itself, a typical day starts at about eight and finishes late. That's hard work! After that, the film is edited[1] and the special effects are put in.
Mag: What do you like best about your work?
ES: I enjoy making the films – and I also enjoy seeing the finished adverts on TV. It's much better than making a whole long film, because you quickly see the results.
Mag: Is there anything you don't like about your work?
ES: Not really, but sometimes I worry about the future. I work for myself, so I always have to look for a new job when a film is finished.
Mag: Where would you like to be in ten years' time?
ES: In America! I love Britain, I grew up here and it's my home. But it's not the best place to make films.

[1]to edit ['edɪt] – *schneiden (Film)*

Your little sister Lara (10) doesn't understand the text. Answer her questions in German.

1. Lara: Wie alt war Emma, als sie wusste, was sie werden will?

   Du: ______________________________

2. Lara: Auf dem Bild sieht sie ein bisschen chinesisch aus. Ist sie Chinesin?

   Du: ______________________________

3. Lara: Wie hat sie ihren Beruf gelernt?

   Du: ______________________________

4. Lara: Sie filmt bestimmt jeden Tag, oder?

   Du: ______________________________

5. Lara: Du hast gemeint, dass sie Fernsehwerbung macht. Warum macht sie keinen Film?

   Du: ______________________________

6. Lara: Das klingt ja genial! Da gibt es bestimmt keine Probleme?

   Du: ______________________________

7. Lara: In zehn Jahren gehe ich nach England und arbeite für sie. Das wäre doch was, oder?

   Du: ______________________________

Green Line 5
ISBN: 978-3-12-547164-1

7 Inversion: An e-mail to an agony aunt

Rewrite the phrases in the box and complete the text.

I didn't think for a moment • I have never in my life been • I have only now decided • It's only then that she returns[1] • She not only comes

Dear Agatha, I have been having a problem for some time, but ____________________ ____________________ that I can't deal with it alone. The problem is my younger sister. ____________________ into my room when I'm not there, but she also borrows my make-up without asking. If I ask her to give it back to me, she just laughs. Then I get really angry. ____________________ my things to me. But that isn't all. I knew she was using my make-up. But ____________________ ____________________ that she was lending it to her friends. ____________________ ____________________ so surprised as I was yesterday, when I came home to find my sister and two friends taking things out of my room. Do you have any advice for me?

[1]to return [rɪ'tɜːn] – *zurückgeben*

8 Emphasis: Going to the cinema

Wherever you see a word in brackets or a gap, give the dialogue more emphasis, e.g. with emphatic forms or with inversion.

Sue: What are you doing this evening?

Polly: I'm going to the cinema with Ian. We're going to watch *Take it Easy*. It's a really (real) good film – at least, that's what I've heard.

Sue: That's for over-sixteens, isn't it?

Polly: That's right. ____________ (I'm) sixteen – remember? Ian isn't sixteen yet, but he ____________ (asked) his mum and dad, and they said he could watch it. His dad says ____________ the scene with the fight ____________ they don't want young people to see. He's seen it ________self, and he doesn't think it would be bad for Ian, but he ____________ (said) that I ________self might have a problem with it, as I'm a girl. He seems to think I'm ____________ (extreme) sensitive.

Sue: And what do you think?

Polly: Well, we'll see. I ____________ (hope) there isn't too much blood and violence. ____________ I'd really like to watch is *Ballet for Two* in the West End next Saturday.

Green Line 5
ISBN: 978-3-12-547164-1

Not ______________________ (be) the premiere, but also Kate Winslet ________self will be there. But that's a dream.

Sue: Yes, I'm afraid you're right. And anyway, _______________ the film ____________'s important, not the people who are there.

Polly: I don't agree. I'm going to watch *Take it Easy* because I enjoy being with Ian. The film _________self isn't important to me.

9 Simple form – progressive form

Complete the gaps with simple and progressive forms in the present, past or present perfect.

Mum knocks on Daniel's door and comes in.

M: Are you still sitting (you/still/sit) there in front of that computer?

D: What do you mean, 'still'? I ______________________________ (not/play) on the computer for very long – only an hour. If you remember, when you came in two hours ago I ____________________ (do) my homework. And please don't say I have to stop now. I ______________________ (just/start) a new game and I _________________ (have) a great time. I ____________ (need) computer games – they help me to relax.

M: Wait a minute. Two hours ago I ________________ (come) in here and you were sitting exactly where you are now – in front of the computer.

D: Yes, I ____________________ (look) on the Internet for some information for History.

M: Hmm – OK, I ________________ (believe) you. I thought you _________________ (play) a computer game. But look outside: the sun ____________________ (shine) – it's such a nice day. You __________________________ (not/be) outside all day.

D: Yes, I have. I've been to school and back.

M: Well, OK, but since you got back you ___________________ (be) in the house.

D: Yes, Mum. I've been doing my homework. What's the problem?

M: It's just that when I ________________ (be) a girl, we used to play outside more.

D: OK, I ____________________ (hear) enough. Mum, I'm sorry, but you __________________________ (stand) here for five minutes and I want to go on with this game. Actually, I've arranged to play football with the other guys at five. Happy now?

M: Why ____________________________ (you/not/tell) me that five minutes ago?

Green Line 5
ISBN: 978-3-12-547164-1

10 Revision: Present and past forms

Complete the dialogue with the correct tense of the verbs.

Jack: Hi, Linda, ______________________________ (you/ever/be) to California?

Linda: No, I ______________________________ (not/be/there/yet). But I ______________________ (think) about going there for a long time, I think I'll go there next year. What about you? ______________________ (you/be) there?

Jack: Yeah, I ____________ (go) to California last year. I ____________ (stay) near Los Angeles.

Linda: Tell me, what ______________________ (you/see?)

Jack: Well, I ____________ (visit) the film studios, of course. You know, I love films and I ______________________________ (always/want) to see where all those famous films ______________________ (be made).

Linda: That must ________________ (be) great. I'm sure you ____________ (take) a lot of photos. Can you ____________ (show) me some?

Jack: Sure, but unfortunately I ________________________ (not/have) time to sort them all. So they're still on the picture card in my digital camera. But I ________________ (promise), I'll do that over the weekend.

Linda: Great. Call me when you __________ ________________ (be/finish), and we'll have a nice evening looking at your photos.

11 Find the missing words

1. You can ____________ the wall with photos or pictures.
2. The songs and music make up the sound ____________ of a movie.
3. The news is on ____________ every night.
4. If you want to show a room in a movie, you often take a ____________ shot.
5. Someone who watches a movie is called a ____________.
6. In a sentence that begins with "Not only …" you must use ____________.

Green Line 5
ISBN: 978-3-12-547164-1

12 Definitions

Write your own definitions for these words.

1. source: ______________________________
2. gossip: ______________________________
3. catch phrase: ______________________________
4. to busk: ______________________________
5. close-up: ______________________________
6. to summarize: ______________________________

13 Adjectives from participles?

Choose the verbs from the box and complete the text with their participles.

animate • design • develop • download • finish • give • know • visit

Today, anybody can successfully create their own little movie. You just need a computer and probably some recently __________ software. With the __________ technology and software you can easily make a computer __________ video. You can even add your personally __________ sound effects, for example by taking a piece of well-__________ music from the Internet and changing it. But be careful with copyrights! If you want to, you can put your __________ video on one of the frequently __________ websites and probably get into the list of __________ video files.

14 ⟨How a song is made⟩

Complete the text with the right words.

It takes a lot of people a lot of time and work before you can __________ to a piece of music. First someone must have a good idea for the __________ and the lyrics of a song. Then they start with the first __________. The __________ and the music are saved on different __________ on a recorder, but often they'll have to __________ __________ mistakes to make it sound perfect. Some special __________ __________ may also be added. When the song is good enough, they have to try to __________ it on the radio or on the Internet. And if that is successful, the song will sell and get into the __________.

Green Line 5
ISBN: 978-3-12-547164-1

15 How to: Argue politely

Write a short, polite dialogue between Jane and Donald. Jane thinks downloading music from the Internet illegally is fun. Donald argues against it.

Jane: I downloaded ______

Donald: ______

Jane: ______

Donald: ______

Jane: ______

Donald: ______

Jane: ______

Donald: ______

16 Mixed bags

a) *Connectives and prepositions: Fill in the missing words.*

Before ______ Susan started her career ______ a singer, she tried to find out ______ she was good enough. ______ she went ______ a studio and asked them to do some recordings[1] with her some time. ______ she was a nice, good-looking girl, the boss told her that the could do it that day. ______ Susan had a cold, she said yes, ______ the result that her voice sounded terrible. ______ of that the people ______ the studio told her she would never become a singer. ______ Susan knew they were wrong and ______ she took part ______ a casting show. ______ she had chosen a good song ______ her voice, she won and got a chance to sing in a band.

b) *Put the verbs in the right tenses and forms.*

In the past people ______ (not/have) as many opportunities for collecting information as we ______ (have) today. During the last 15 years there ______ (be) a revolution in information technology. Just imagine: 20 years ago the fastest way to get a message to a far-away place ______ (be) the telephone. And whenever you ______ (want) to send something in written form, you ______ (have to/do) it by post. Today one only ______ (have to/go) to one's computer, send an e-mail, and the addressee[2] ______ (have) the document in no time.

[1]recording [rɪ'kɔːdɪŋ] – *Aufnahme*, [2]addressee [ˌædres'iː] – *Adressat*

Green Line 5
ISBN: 978-3-12-547164-1

Unit 4 Human rights

1 Listening: The freedom of the press

a) *Listen to a phone call. Which pictures match the dialogue? Tick (✔).*

1 ☐

2 ☐

3 ☐

4 ☐

5 ☐

6 ☐

7 ☐

8 ☐

b) *Answer the questions with 1–6 words. You needn't write full sentences.*

1. Who is Paul Smith? ______________________________
2. What was listed in the article about him? ______________________________
3. Who took the photo of Paul Smith's wedding[1]? ______________________________
4. Which right does Paul Smith mention? ______________________________
5. What are informed citizens[2] able to make? ______________________________
6. Where did Paul Smith celebrate the wedding?

   ____
7. What is more important for Larry Miller than the right to privacy?

   ____
8. What did different magazines ask Paul Smith to do?

   ____
9. Why doesn't Larry Miller want to pay for the photo of the wedding?

   ____

[1]wedding ['wedɪŋ] – celebration when getting married, [2]citizen ['sɪtɪzn] – *Bürger/in*

Green Line 5
ISBN: 978-3-12-547164-1

2 Understanding films: Facing challenges

Which sentence goes with which picture? Watch the film and draw lines to the right picture.

1

Leave a message on my cell phone.

I'll take care of your Internet.

4

2

I need a table at the Four Seasons.

The Four Seasons is booked out tonight.

5

3

Do you think I'm stupid?

I have no idea how to make a reservation.

6

3 Reading: Stop and search[1]

When Jack Davies was walking home one day he suddenly saw two police officers coming towards him. When they stopped in front of him, he politely asked if he could pass, but their answer was "no". Instead of letting Jack continue on his way, the police officers asked him to empty his pockets and take his baseball cap off. But Jack refused[2].

"Under the powers given to us by Code A to the Police and Criminal Evidence[3] Act of 1984, we're stopping you to search you," one of the police officers said. "You are suspected of[4] being a member of a gang of drug dealers. We need to search you to find out if you are carrying any drugs," she added.

"But I'm not a member of any gang and I don't even know what you are talking about!" Jack replied. "I don't think this is the real reason for you stopping me, I think it's because I'm black, isn't it?!"

"It certainly is not," said her male colleague, "and now, please do as you were told and empty your pockets!" Jack did not react. The two officers stepped closer. The man grabbed Jack's arms and held them tightly while the woman took Jack's baseball cap off his head and started to empty his pockets. Jack fought to free himself but it was two against one; no chance. Inside his pockets they found some money and keys but, as Jack had said, no sign of any drugs. And the money was not enough to be from dealing. Looking a little frustrated, the female officer dropped what she had found on the ground, along with the baseball cap. The other officer let go of Jack's arms. They then turned round and walked off without another word, leaving Jack both angry and confused[5].

FACTS ON 'stop and search'

- The police have the power to stop and search people suspected of crimes under the Police and Criminal Evidence Act of 1984.
- There must be good reasons for searching a person.
- The police must show fairness in choosing the people they stop; stopping people must not be based on reasons of discrimination.
- Unfortunately, there is often discrimination in the use of powers, as black people are five times more likely to be searched than whites.

Green Line 5
ISBN: 978-3-12-547164-1

When Jack woke up the next morning, his arms still in pain, he decided to see the local social worker, a young man he had confidence in, and complain about how the police officers had behaved. He told him the whole story and ended by saying, "I think I was only being discriminated against[6] because of my skin color." "No, you weren't," the social worker replied, "the police do have a right to stop and search people if they are suspected of being involved in a crime." "But I wasn't!" Jack protested. "Very well, but how should the police know if they don't check it out? I have to admit though," the social worker said, "that before doing anything else, they should have explained to you what was going on and what they wanted from you. But after *not* doing what you had been asked to do the first time, the police officers had no choice but to hold your arms and empty your pockets *for* you. They couldn't wait for *you* to decide to cooperate[7] when you feel like it; you might have had a gun and tried to shoot them, so they had to act quickly. They were only doing their job, but I'm sorry they didn't tell you sooner why they had stopped you. No wonder you felt discriminated against."

[1]to search [sɜːtʃ] – *durchsuchen*, [2]to refuse [rɪ'fjuːz] – to say no, [3]evidence ['evɪdns] – *Beweis*, [4]to suspect sb of sth [sə'spekt] – *jmdn. einer Sache verdächtigen*, [5]confused [kən'fjuːzd] – not knowing what to think of sth, [6]to discriminate against sb [dɪ'skrɪmɪneɪt] – to treat sb badly because of race, sex or age, [7]to cooperate [kəʊ'ɒpreɪt] – to work together

a) *In which line(s) do you find the information?*

1. Jack didn't want to get into trouble. line 2
2. The police have the power to stop and search people. ______
3. The officers thought Jack might be involved in drug dealing. ______
4. Jack isn't white. ______
5. The officers searched Jack against his will. ______
6. The officers didn't find what they were looking for. ______
7. The next day Jack's arms still hurt. ______
8. The social worker explained to Jack what the police did. ______
9. Although they have the right to search people, the officers could have behaved better. ______

b) *Put the events in the right order.*

- ☐ Jack talks to the social worker.
- ☐ The policemen stop Jack.
- ☐ Jack wakes up with his arms hurting.
- ☐ Jack walks home.
- ☐ One of the officers empties Jack's pockets while the other one holds his arms.
- ☐ Jack asks the officers to let him pass.

Green Line 5
ISBN: 978-3-12-547164-1

4 Writing: A newspaper article

Jack reports to a journalist what happened to him. The reporter, who is interested in human rights stories, writes an article and puts Jack right at the centre of it.

Write the article and think of a headline that catches the reader's attention.

5 Speaking: Human rights

Choose the photo that – in your opinion – shows the problem of violation (Verletzung) of human rights best. Prepare a short talk to the class on why you have chosen that photo and what its message is.

Green Line 5
ISBN: 978-3-12-547164-1

6 Mediation: An important figure of the human rights movement

Situation: Your English friend sees the article in a book titled 'Menschenrechte'. All she can understand is that it is about Martin Luther King and she asks you what the article says about him.

Im Jahr 1929 wurde einer der bekanntesten Bürgerrechtler der Vereinigten Staaten von Amerika geboren: Martin Luther King. Er machte den Kampf gegen die Rassentrennung zu seinem Lebensinhalt und feierte als führender Repräsentant der Bürgerrechtsbewegung zahlreiche Erfolge gegen die damals bestehenden Gesetze. So erlangten unter seiner Führung die Schwarzen das Wahlrecht und die Trennung von Schwarzen und Weißen, beispielsweise in Schulen, wurde aufgehoben. Im Mittelpunkt seiner Bemühungen stand für Martin Luther King stets der friedliche Protest und so führte er 1963 250 000 Menschen in einem Protestmarsch nach Washington D.C., wo er eine bewegende Rede mit dem Titel „I have a dream" hielt. Sein Vorgehen brachte ihm zugleich zahlreiche Feinde, sogar in den eigenen Reihen, da ihm vorgeworfen wurde, nicht mit mehr Gewalt für die Rechte der Schwarzen zu kämpfen. Im Alter von nur 39 Jahren wurde Martin Luther King 1968 von einem Attentäter erschossen, sein Traum von einem Land ohne Rassismus allerdings besteht bis heute fort.

Tell your friend in English what you have learned about Martin Luther King from the article.

ISBN: 978-3-12-547164-1

7 Fill in the right prepositions

Michael had been interested ________ joining the police since he was a little boy. He had always looked forward ________ becoming a police officer himself, but when he found out that some officers use their legal power ________ stop and search[1] people ______________ having a good reason, he began ________ have second thoughts ______________ his dream job. He didn't want to work __________ people who would discriminate against[2] others, e.g. because ________ the colour of their skin. Now, many years later, Michael is a teenager preparing ________ A-Levels. When asked ______________ his career ideas for the future, his reply ________ that question is always the same: He wants to become a lawyer more than anything else. That would give him the chance to help people who have got __________ trouble __________ the police.

[1]to search [sɜːtʃ] – *durchsuchen*, [2]to discriminate against sb [dɪ'skrɪmɪneɪt]– to treat sb badly because of race, sex or age

8 Gerund or infinitive

Fill in the right forms.

We are quite lucky _________________ (live) in a country where human rights are protected[1] by law. In some countries people are not allowed _______________________ (speak) about political or social issues in public. And if they are caught ______________________ (criticize) the government, they might go to prison. Human rights organizations try __________________ (support) the people in prison, but they are often not allowed ____________________ (enter) the country. And if they are able __________ (get) into the country, they are often stopped from ______________________ (get into) contact with the political prisoners. We should never stop ________________________ (think) about how __________________ (stop) the infringement[2] of people's rights.

[1]to protect [prə'tekt] – *(be)schützen*, [2]infringement [ɪn'frɪndʒmənt] – *Verletzung*

9 Verbs

*Fill in the right forms of the verbs – infinitive or gerund. Sometimes **to** might be needed.*

1. Jenny always used __________________ (be) blonde; now she has dark hair.
2. As a child, Jake had always looked forward __________________ (go) away on holiday with his family.
3. Emma can't stand __________________ (be) alone in the dark.
4. When she was young, Tina was only interested in __________________ (go) out.

Green Line 5
ISBN: 978-3-12-547164-1

5. After the death of his wife, Mr Turner never stopped ________________ (think) of her.

6. Sometimes it's hard for parents ________________ (understand) their child's feelings.

7. Sorry, I didn't mean ________________ (hurt) you by ________________ (say) you were an idiot.

8. If you want to be famous, you need fans to help you ________________ (become) a star.

10 Indirect speech

Remember Jack Davies who was stopped and searched[1] by two police officers? Here is a part of the conversation between Jack and the social worker he spoke to after the event. A few days later the street worker tells the story to a friend.

Report the conversation.

Jack: I was just on my way home when the police officers stopped me without any obvious reason. I was asked to take off my cap and empty[2] my pockets.

Jack told me ____

____

Social worker: How many police officers were there?

I asked ____

Jack: There were two of them and they were very rude. When I didn't do as I was told, one of them grabbed my arms and the other one took my cap and threw everything I had in my pockets on the ground.

____

____

____

Social worker: Did they tell you why you were stopped and searched?

____

Jack: Not until I asked. Then they said that I was suspected of[3] being a member of a gang of drug dealers. But I'd never do that kind of thing! The two only let go of me after they realized I wasn't carrying any drugs. But now I've really lost confidence in the police.

____

____

____

____

[1]to search [sɜːtʃ] – *durchsuchen*, [2]to empty ['empti] – to take everything out of sth,
[3]to suspect sb of sth [sə'spekt] – *jmdn. einer Sache verdächtigen*

Green Line 5
ISBN: 978-3-12-547164-1

11 Modals and their substitutes

Sandy and her friend Tina talk about the summer holidays. Before making plans for a trip together, Sandy tells her friend about the horrible holidays she had the year before.

Fill in the correct substitutes.

Sandy: Last summer I ____________ (must) go to Spain for the summer holidays because my parents said my grades in Spanish were too bad.

Tina: Oh, really? To Spain? ____________ (you/cannot) go anywhere else – like Costa Rica?

Sandy: No, they wouldn't let me. I even ____________ (must) go all on my own and ____________ (must/not) take a friend.

Tina: And ____________ (you/must) study a lot then?

Sandy: Yes! It was horrible. I ____________ (cannot) get enough sleep because the lessons started so early in the morning. We ____________ (may) go to the cinema only once a week but we ____________ (may/not) go to a disco or a youth club. And the worst thing was that I ____________ (cannot) take the plane but ____________ (must) go by bus as my parents said going by plane was too expensive!

Tina: Our trip this year will definitely be a lot better, I promise! We ____________ (can) do a lot of funny things and not ask anyone!

12 How to: Show everyday courage and support

What could you say in the following situations? Remember to address the people involved appropriately.

1. In a toy shop: The shop assistant has just shown you a toy that is very cheap. You find out that it was made by small children in India. You don't think toys like this should be sold at all.

____

____

____

____

____

Green Line 5
ISBN: 978-3-12-547164-1

2. At a school: You see two young white girls hitting and kicking a little black girl and calling her racist names. You want them to stop.

____

____

____

____

____

13 Crossword

Across: →
5. the noun form of 'to integrate'
8. a system of keeping different parts of society separate from each other
9. a different word for 'homosexual'
10. showing that you disagree something, for example with a march
12. people who don't have a place to live

Down: ↓
1. the parliament of the United States
2. people who are involved in … must go to prison
3. a society in which people elect the politicians
4. Journalists' work is only safe if there's … of the Press.
6. the noun form of 'racial'
7. a condition in which people have no control of their lives and have to work for others without payment
11. the verb form of 'tolerance'

Green Line 5
ISBN: 978-3-12-547164-1

14 Phrases

Match the verbs with the phrases in the box. Find the best pairs.

a difference • a different opinion • a good education • a law • child labour • as perfect • a problem • soldiers • to the waiter • your mind

1. to change ____________________
2. to complain ____________________
3. to handle ____________________
4. to make ____________________
5. to pass ____________________
6. to qualify ____________________
7. to receive ____________________
8. to recruit ____________________
9. to ban ____________________
10. to tolerate ____________________

15 Mixed bag: Human rights

Fill in the missing words. Choose from the box.

appropriate • attention • bullied • child labour • considered to • democratic • developing world • dignity • equal • improve • in spite of • to integrate • position of power • slavery • speak out about • target

One of the basic principles[1] of our ____________________ society is that all men and women are created ____________. In contrast, in the ____________________ ____________, minorities still have problems ______ ____________________ and even segregation might still be an issue. ______ ____________ ______ laws granting[2] racial equality in some of those countries, people continue to be treated without the ____________________ respect. Those in a ____________ ______ ____________ sometimes use their regime to put many poor people in work situations close to ______________. Minorities can become the ______________ of racist attacks and their lives are often ____________________ ______ be of less value. In other countries ____________ ______________ is a big issue as the young workers are often ______________ into working in sweatshops under awful conditions[3], where children lose the last bit of ______________ they might still have had. To ______________ the human rights situation, one should ______________ ________ ____________ the existing problems and that way bring other people's ______________ to the issue.

[1]principle ['prɪnsəpl] – *Prinzip*, [2]to grant [grɑːnt] – *garantieren*, [3]condition [kən'dɪʃn] – *Bedingung*

Green Line 5
ISBN: 978-3-12-547164-1

Lösungen

Unit 1 Australia

1 Listening: Australian crocodiles

Text:

Woman: I'm really nervous about the outback. I've heard that there are some really dangerous animals out there. Are you really sure it's safe for us to go?

Man: Why? Are your afraid a kangaroo might hop on you?

Woman: Come on, what about dingoes?

Man: Can I tell you a secret? Aussies love telling tourists scary stories about animals in the Outback. But the truth is that most of the animals in the outback won't hurt you and are probably just as scared of you.

Woman: Not the dingoes. They're aggressive.

Man: They really never attack people.

Woman: And what about spiders?

Man: More people die in Australia because they are allergic to bee stings! Really you just have to use your head. If you really want to see a dangerous animal, you should …

Woman: I didn't say I wanted to!

Man: … you should go to the northern coast of Australia. There are more dangerous animals in the water around Australia than on land.

Woman: Well of course I want to see the coast. Sandy beaches, big waves, beautiful sunsets …

Man: Saltwater crocodiles, box jellyfish, blue-ringed octopus …

Woman: What are you talking about now?

Man: Dangerous animals – that's what you wanted to talk about, wasn't it?

Woman: Ha ha. OK, Mr Know-it-all. What do you want to tell me about now? I know that things don't happen like in the movie Jaws about the great white shark.

Man: Well, for your information, about one person a year dies from an attack from a great white shark.

Woman: Sounds like enough to me.

Man: The saltwater crocodiles are actually much more dangerous.

Woman: Then we'll just stay in the fresh water.

Man: Um, actually they live in fresh water, too. Their name is kind of …

Woman: Oh great!

Man: Yeah, and actually they are the most dangerous animals in Australia, but if you're careful then …

Woman: Then what?

Man: You just have to be careful and follow the rules. Stay away from rivers and any deep and still waters. Crocodiles hide just below the top of the water and attack when something gets close.

Woman: And if we're in a boat?

Man: You have to be careful there, too. Don't put your arms or legs over the side of the boat.

Woman: And how many people die each year?

Man: Only about one or two people in Australia die from crocodile attacks each year, although there are a lot more attacks.

Woman: Only … I guess I'll stay in the outback and be safe and forget the coast.

a) 2. wrong; 3. right; 4. right; 5. right; 6. wrong; 7. wrong; 8. right

b) Know-it-all, movie, white, person a year, enough, much more dangerous, stay

c) 1. C; 2. A; 3. B; 4. B

2 Understanding films: Choosing a career

1. For a hotel manager lots of different skills are important.
2. Before you can be a hotel manager, you have to do a 3-year course.
3. A work placement is a good way to find out if a career is right for you.
4. During a work placement you learn about the positive and negative aspects of a job.
5. The careers adviser suggests a work placement in a hotel in Germany.
6. She tells Maya to contact an office in Central London.
7. Maya thinks that something was wrong with her outfit.
8. It doesn't make a good impression to arrive late for an interview.

3 Reading: Movie reviews: *Australia*, 2008

a) 2. right; 3. right; 4. right; 5. right; 6. not in the text; 7. wrong; 8. right; 9. wrong; 10. not in the text; 11. right; 12. wrong

b) 2. Stolen Generation/Japanese attack on Darwin. 3. He drives cattle. 4. There are three storylines. 5. In Australia. 6. A good story. 7. Her husband has been killed. 8. They hate each other. 9. An opposites-attract love story. 10. You can read a good book.

4 Writing: Better safe than sorry

Individuelle Lösungen

5 Speaking: About Australia

Individuelle Vorträge

Green Line 5
ISBN: 978-3-12-547164-1

6 Mediation: Salties

1. *Salzwasserkrokodile findet man an den Küsten Australiens, nördlich der südlichen Tropen, und bis mehr als 100 km ins Landesinnere hinein. Allein im Northern Territory gibt es ungefähr 85000 und weitere Zehntausende in Queensland und Westaustralien.*
2. *– Möglichst nicht nachts unterwegs sein, weil Krokodile nachts aktiv sind.*
   – Trinkstellen von Tieren meiden, denn dort warten Krokodile gern auf Beute.
   – Beim Campen niemals Essen oder Müll herumliegen lassen, denn der Geruch könnte Krokodile anlocken.
   – Niemals ein Krokodil provozieren, sondern vielmehr ruhig bleiben, wenn man eines sieht.
   – Wo sich Warnschilder befinden, niemals ins Wasser gehen, auch wenn man kein Krokodil sieht.

7 Gracey and Angela

who, (comma) who (comma after 'Gracey'), –, (comma) whose (comma after 'rally'), which, –, (comma) which (comma after 'cool'), which

8 The Great Barrier Reef

1. The Great Barrier Reef, which begins just off the coast of Bundaberg and extends1 over 2,000 km north to western Papua New Guinea, is one of the natural wonders of the world.
2. It is in fact not a single reef, but a collection of over 2,900 individual reefs, 300 coral cays and 600 continental islands full of life, colour and adventure.
3. The Great Barrier Reef Marine Park, which covers over 98% of the area, was opened in 1975.
4. Here's an example of a damaged coral (that) you can find at the Great Barrier Reef.
5. The green season, which provides 75–90% of the region's rainfall, starts with the first of the monsoon rains in November and ends in May.

9 The next day

let, have, made, let, let, made, have, make, made, have, making

10 Situations

2. Her friend is making her cut her hair.
3. The Smiths are having their milk delivered.
4. His parents are letting Steve go on a school exchange to Australia.
5. Dean's dad is making the teenagers listen to him.
6. Milly is letting Daisy play with her teddy bear.

11 Life back then from 1901 to 1914

1. "Life back then **used to be** really hard. I had to work under bad conditions and the work itself was dangerous. People **used to be** afraid for their health. I **used to earn** just A$5.50 and for that I had to work a 50-hour week!"
2. "Today I am often asked: 'Did you really **use to work** that hard? Did you have to work so many hours?'"
3. "Today's young people just can't believe it. You see, it **didn't use to be** like today. We **used to work** like dogs to put food on the table. Nowadays life is easier for workers but it wouldn't be if we hadn't fought for it in earlier times. We pushed for higher pay and better working conditions."
4. "My house was quite small and as we **used to work** all day, we had little time for leisure activities."
5. "Australia **used to have** six separate colonies, but in 1901 the colonies became one nation. It was then governed by just one Federation. We became the Commonwealth of Australia."
6. "We celebrated the Federation across the nation and had a good time. We **didn't use to be** a multicultural society back then. The population **used to be** mainly people directly from the British Isles or Australian-born white lads. A lot of people **used to see** Britain as their home and education **used to be** influenced by British beliefs."

12 How to: Explain a problem on the train

Lösungsvorschlag:

You: My rucksack and all my money was stolen.
Man: Did you notice anything?
You: No, I'm afraid not. May I use your mobile phone for a quick call? I promise it won't take long?
Man: Do you have the number of the German consulate?
You: No, I'd like to call the police.
Man: There is a police officer on this train.
You: Could you help me, please? My rucksack was stolen.
Police officer: May I see your passport?
You: It was in my rucksack.
Police officer: Please fill out these forms so that I can help you. The German consulate can give you a new passport for your flight home.

13 Find the odd one out

1. koala: It's not a dangerous animal.
2. perspective: Its second letter isn't 'r'.
3. Aboriginal: It's not a nationality.
4. ancestor: It's not a person who has broken the law.

Green Line 5
ISBN: 978-3-12-547164-1

14 Word power

1. all the countries in the eastern part of the world that have a Pacific coast
2. the wild, empty country away from Australia's towns and cities
3. a country convicts are sent to
4. not from your own country
5. a list of questions with which you can find out about people's opinions
6. a slang/colloquial expression to describe a person from Australia
7. somebody who thinks somebody else is not his/her equal just because the other person's skin colour/race is different

15 Find the right words

Down: 1. worry-wart; 3. democracy; 4. Aborigines; 5. exotic; 6. platypus
Across: 2. borrow; 7. ozone layer; 8. forest

16 Fill in the right words

excited, penal, prisoners, made, convicts, made, heavy, dangerous, had, stealing, used to, Asia, Asian-Pacific, activities, surfing, outback, said, crocodile, supposed, animals, shark

17 Mixed bag: The Stolen Generation

who, who, who, who, up, not, in, who, turn/change, person/child, that, to be, them, why, was, been, his, (that), been, ran, next, in, playing, for, good, songs

Zusätzlicher Text für das Hörverstehen: Henry is visiting Edward in Australia

Henry: I don't want to walk through those trees and bushes. There might be some dangerous animals in there.
Edward: Like what?
Henry: Like a snake[1]. A brown snake maybe. I've read about them. They're deadly[2]. People are killed every year.
Edward: Yes, but you have to be lucky to find them. They aren't all over Australia, you know?
Henry: Yes, but there are other dangerous snakes and spiders.
Edward: Oh Henry. But animals don't want to meet us. When they hear us, they'll move away. They only attack you if you scare[3] them.
Henry: Well, I'll talk to them nicely then.
Edward: Come on. We'll see some beautiful birds here and we can go swimming in the river.
Henry: In the river?
Edward: Yes! And before you ask, no ... there aren't any crocodiles in it.
Henry: OK.
Edward: Hey, what was that?
Henry: Ow. Ow. My leg! A snake has bitten[4] me. Look. Look at that blood!
Edward: Let me look!
Henry: I saw it. It was a snake and it was brown. Call an ambulance. I don't want to die.
Edward: You won't die. Just sit still and you will be OK soon.
Henry: What are you doing? Where are you going?
Edward: I'm looking for your snake.
Henry: You're looking for what? Why? Are you crazy? It might bite you, too.
Edward: No, no. It won't. ... Look here! I've found it.
Henry: What is it? What bit me?
Edward: This.
Henry: That?
Edward: Yes.
Henry: But that's a stick!
Edward: Yes, a brown stick, with your blood on the end.
Henry: But sticks don't bite!
Edward: No! But they can hurt your leg.
Henry: Oh! So you mean there was no snake?
Edward: No!
Henry: But that's one there in that tree behind your head.
Edward: Where? Where? Oh, it was a joke.

[1]snake [sneɪk] – *Schlange,* [2]deadly ['dedli] – *tödlich,* [3]to scare [skeə] – *ängstigen,* [4]to bite [baɪt] – *beißen*

Zusätzlicher Text für das Leseverstehen: Death or the First Fleet

Paula Dawson, from London, is one of many tourists in Sydney. She is in a museum. She has just stopped in front of a huge poster that has been put up in the main hall. It shows a timeline and information about the convicts who were taken to Australia on the so-called[1] First Fleet[2]. Paula notices a name: Margaret Dawson, from London. Her grandad had talked about a 'Margaret' in Sydney years ago. Could this 'Margaret Dawson' maybe be someone from her family tree? Paula starts her tour. She switches on[3] her headphones[4] and listens to Margaret's story: "Margaret Dawson was a convict. She was also one of the first mothers of this country and so helped to found Australia. She was born in Liverpool in 1770. When she was 15, she worked in a rich family's house in London. We do not know if the family were fair to her or if they made her work too hard and gave her very little money. But one day she stole some clothes, jewellery and money from their home and tried to get back to Liverpool. She was caught on the way and got the death sentence[5]! But this sentence was changed because she had never stolen

Green Line 5
ISBN: 978-3-12-547164-1

before and because she was so young. She got a seven-year sentence – to be transported to the new colony at Sydney Cove. The journey was long and terrible. Her new life was hard but there was no way to escape[6]. Towards the end of her sentence she met a doctor, William Balmain – perhaps while she was looking after sick convicts who arrived later on the Second Fleet. When her sentence ended in 1793, we know that she could read and write and that she was a farmer. How do we know this? Well, she bought some farm goods[7] at the official store and signed for them. And we still have this sheet of paper[8]. She and the doctor and their two children left Sydney in August 1801 and sailed for London. Margaret Dawson could never marry William because she had been a convict. We know they had another baby, who was born in London. But very little is known about this child. One of the older children became a doctor like his father. Margaret Dawson died in February 1816."

[1]so-called [ˈsəʊkɔːld] – *so genannt,* [2]fleet [fliːt] – *Flotte,* [3]to switch on [swɪtʃ‿ˈɒn] – *einschalten,* [4]headphones [ˈhedfəʊnz] – *Kopfhörer,* [5]death sentence [ˈdeθ ˌsentəns] – *Todesstrafe,* [6]to escape [ɪˈskeɪp] – *entkommen,* [7]goods [gʊdz] – *Waren,* [8]sheet of paper [ˌʃiːt‿əv ˈpeɪpə] – *Blatt Papier*

Unit 2 What next?

1 Listening: Careers talk

Text:

Teacher: OK. Sit down, please. Now – as most of you know, I'm the careers' teacher at this school. At some time during this year you will all be able to come and see me and talk about your ideas on a career. Now I know that most of you have no idea which career you would like to choose … and so what I want to do today is show you what's important to think about while you're deciding, and what you can do to help yourself. So first of all what do you think the most important thing is to think about when you're choosing a career?

Peter: How much it pays, sir.

Teacher: OK. OK. Well, Peter. That is important. Of course, it is. If you want to become an artist or an actor, for example, you have to know that it's very difficult to get a job and that often when you do get a job, it pays very badly. So if you want a big car or you want to go on holiday every year, then maybe you should think about something else. And, of course, you definitely shouldn't become a teacher.

Peter: Very good, sir. Very good joke. Ha ha.

Teacher: But OK. What is more important than that? What do you need to think about first?

Lisa: Well, you have to decide what your talents are.

Teacher: Yes, Lisa. That's very important. If you aren't good at doing something, then nobody will pay you to do it.

Ryan: And you have to think about what you like doing.

Teacher: Yes, Ryan. You spend a lot of time working and so it's important that you enjoy it. And if you enjoy doing something, you can become better at it ... even if you aren't so good now. So, for a couple of minutes, I'd like you all to write two lists. One of things that you enjoy doing and one of things that you're good at doing.

Peter: Well, I like watching TV and eating, sir.

Teacher: Well, write that down. No, seriously. There are many famous directors who just loved watching TV and films when they were younger. They loved it so much that they learned more about it and in the end they were able to do it as a job. … OK. Have you all finished?

Peter: No, sir. I'm still writing down all my talents.

Teacher: Yes, well, maybe you could finish it off after the lesson. ... For anybody who really has problems choosing a career you can go to the careers office and fill in a form about your interests and talents. Then somebody will put all the information about you into a computer programme and the computer will suggest

ISBN: 978-3-12-547164-1

some careers to you. Yes, it sounds a bit strange, I know, but it actually often works. There are so many careers out there – many that I've never even heard of – that there will definitely be one for you. You just need to find it.

a) 2. right; 3. wrong; 4. wrong; 5. wrong; 6. right; 7. wrong; 8. right

b) pictures 2, 3, 5, 8: (film) director, artist, actor, teacher

2 Understanding films: Applying for a job

a) 1. good team work; 2. must be open-minded and flexible; 3. must always be friendly and calm

b) 1. hotel management; 2. assistant manager; 3. with the basics; 4. four months; 5. getting a placement; 6. a hotel in Berlin

3 Reading: Job advertisements on the Internet

a) 1. C; 2. C; 3. B; 4. B; 5. C; 6. A; 7. A; 8. A

b) 1. graphic designer, receptionist 2. graphic designer, receptionist 3. student adviser, graphic designer, ad posting, receptionist 4. graphic designer, general manager

4 Writing: A letter of application

a) *Individuelle Lösungen*
b) *Lösungsvorschlag:*
Application for the job as receptionist
Dear Dr. Cook,
I am writing to apply for the job as a receptionist / medical assistant which you advertised on the Internet. As you will see from the enclosed CV, I have the qualifications you require. I have been a doctor's receptionist in San Diego for two years now, but I am moving to Pasadena soon for personal reasons. I have good communication and computer skills, and I enjoy working with people and helping them. I have a lot of experience with children, and I speak fluent Spanish.
I am sure I will be able to organize your office very successfully.
I would be pleased to come in for an interview at your convenience. I look forward to hearing from you soon.
Yours sincerely,
…
Encl. CV, 2 references

5 Speaking: Work experience

Individuelle Gespräche

6 Mediation: Pupils' reports

1. *Catherine hat in einem Krankenhaus gearbeitet und Rachel in einer Grundschule.*
2. *Alle waren nett zu ihr, sie konnte einigen Patienten helfen, sie lernte viel und traf beeindruckende Leute.*
3. *Die Arbeit im Büro und am Computer.*
4. *Sie durfte bei einer Operation zusehen.*
5. *Catherine kann sich gut vorstellen, einen medizinischen Beruf ergreifen.*
6. *Das Geschichten erzählen/Die Geschichten, die die Schüler erfunden haben.*
7. *Dass sie zu ungeduldig ist, um mit so kleinen Kindern auf Dauer zu arbeiten.*
8. *Rachel würde vielleicht ältere Kinder unterrichten.*
9. *Rachel hat ein gutes Zeugnis erhalten. (Catherine schreibt nichts dazu.)*

7 Relative clauses and participles

1. Students wanting to become engineers often choose a work experience placement in a factory.
2. Some big firms have special programmes planned to help student visitors.
3. Read what one of the young people doing work experience has written in her report.
4. "Most of the work done by the engineers is too difficult for me."
5. "But I'm sure the experiences offered to me here will be very useful in future."

8 An exciting evening at work

After I had had a weekend job in a garage, I wanted a different kind of holiday job.
I found work at a restaurant which was known to be very expensive. One evening, because I had been asked to help one of the waitresses, I was clearing a table. Then I heard sounds which were coming from the table in the corner. When I turned round, I saw two men who were exchanging money and small packets. Because I was shocked by what I had seen, I informed the manager. When they (the police) arrived at the restaurant ten minutes later, the police (they) found more money and drugs which were hidden in the men's shoes.

9 A career as a journalist

Nicole wants to become a journalist, having often worked on the school magazine. She enjoys writing texts informing students and parents about interesting events, and she once reported about plans for new school rules heavily criticised by students. Nicole knows that when trying to get a job with a newspaper, she must have some experience or qualifications making her a suitable person for the job. She often sends short articles to magazines,

Green Line 5
ISBN: 978-3-12-547164-1

hoping that they will be published. After leaving / having left school, Nicole plans to take a creative writing course advertised on all the career websites.

10 What did Gavin see and hear?

1. He watched some children fighting.
2. He heard an ambulance driving along the road.
3. He saw some dogs playing in the park.
4. He listened to two boys talking about football.
5. He noticed two girls sitting under a tree.

11 Talking about the future

'm/am going to be, will give, will always be, 'm/am going to start, 'm/am playing, 'm/am meeting, arrives, 'm/am going to win, 'll/will think

12 How to: Talk about personal qualities

Individuelle Lösungen

13 Which part of the word is stressed?

●•• architect, hairdresser, signature, suitable
•●• appointment, construction, creative, musician, sincerely
••● engineer, guarantee, questionnaire

14 Word families

1. employer; 2. applicants; 3. signature; 4. society; 5. imaginative

15 Different jobs

1. firefighter; 2. engineer; 3. personnel manager; 4. police officer; 5. architect; 6. meteorologist

16 Mixed bag: Linda can't decide

a) on; b) had; c) suit; d) talking; e) fluent; f) lawyer; g) pass; h) mainly; i) recently; j) rises; k) get; l) By; m) likely; n) the

Zusatztext für das Hörverstehen:
A job interview for practice

[First: Interview questions with pauses for S replies]

Interviewer: Good morning. Please take a seat.
S: …
I: I see from your application that you're interested in multimedia. Have you had any work experience?
S: …
I: I see, that sounds very interesting. When will you be taking your A-levels?
S: …
I: And in which subjects?
S: …
I: And why do you think a job in our company would suit you?
S: …
I: Would you like to work your way up in the company?
S: …
I: Can you tell me about your strong points?
S: …
I: And tell me about one weakness you have.
S: …
I: What activities have you been involved in outside of school?
S: …
I: Have you applied to other companies?
S: …
I: Thank you. Do you have any questions for me? I'm sure you've looked at our website.

[Second: Model interview]

Interviewer: Good morning. Please take a seat.
Applicant: Good morning. Thank you.
I: I see from your application that you're interested in multimedia. Have you had any work experience?
A: Yes, I have. I had the opportunity to work at a TV station last summer for one month. I worked in the graphic design department and got a very good impression of the work.
I: I see, that sounds very interesting. When will you be taking your A-levels?
A: I am taking my A-levels in May.
I: And in which subjects?
A: My exams will be in German, Maths and History.
I: And why do you think a job in our company would suit you?
A: Preparing for my job search, I learned that your company is growing quickly and offers many opportunities for younger people. You have contacts around the world giving me the impression that I would also be able to use my language skills.
I: Would you like to work your way up in the company?
A: Yes, I would like to work my way up. I believe that challenges are important and help you improve.

Green Line 5
ISBN: 978-3-12-547164-1

Making plans for myself is something that I have always done.

I: Can you tell me about your strong points?

A: I'm hard-working and always finish what I've started. Deadlines aren't a problem for me because I can manage my work and get it done on time – on my own or in a team.

I: And tell me about one weakness you have.

A: Saying "no" is sometimes difficult for me. For example, if someone asks me to help with a new project. First of all I enjoy helping and secondly I like trying new things. But sometimes saying "no" would be better because there isn't enough time to do everything.

I: What activities have you been involved in outside of school?

A: I help with charity campaigns in my town and I play on the town field hockey team.

I: Have you applied to other companies?

A: Yes, I think it's important to apply to different kinds of companies – big and small ones, for example. I've applied to eight other companies in the area.

I: Thank you. Do you have any questions for me? I'm sure you've looked at our website.

A: What per cent of your customers comes from countries outside Britain and how do you advise them?

Zusatztext für das Leseverstehen:
A personal statement

At the moment I am studying Maths, Chemistry and Information Technology at A Level. I have found all the subjects interesting so far, but the one I enjoy most is IT. The course covers[1] a number of technical topics, from programming languages to graphic design. Because of my interest in computers, I am thinking of doing Software Engineering at university.
At the end of year ten I did a one-week work placement with a company called SunSpot Electronics. While I was there, they were developing solar energy technology and my job was to support the engineers. It was a very enjoyable, interesting and educational[2] time, and I discovered that I had a talent for working in a project team.
As well as studying for my A Levels, I belong to[3] our school website group. I helped to design our homepage and created graphics for it. We are developing an online learning program called the Virtual Classroom. Tests will be starting soon, but unfortunately I will have left school by the time it is ready to use.
I am also involved in charity events. In April I will be taking part in a sponsored bicycle ride[4] from London to Cambridge to raise money for 'Help the Homeless'. The number of homeless[5] people is rising, and I feel a duty to help them.
As far as my hobbies are concerned[6], I enjoy writing and performing electronic music. I have been a member of a band for seven months now, and we will be having our first concert soon. I am also a good swimmer and have won several[7] medals with the school team. I hope I will be able to carry on[8] with these hobbies at university.
I also enjoy travelling. Two years ago I took part in an exchange programme with our partner school in Germany. This summer I will be visiting Australia to meet my grandparents for the first time. I am looking forward to starting university and I hope I will enjoy it as much as I have enjoyed being at school.

[1]to cover ['kʌvə] – *hier: umfassen,* [2]educational [ˌedʒʊ'keɪʃnl] – *bildend,* [3]to belong to [bɪ'lɒŋ tə] – *gehören zu,* [4]bicycle ride ['baɪsɪkl ˌraɪd] – *Fahrradtour,* [5]homeless ['həʊmlɪs] – *obdachlos,* [6]as far as … is/are concerned [kən'sɜːnd] – *was … betrifft,* [7]several ['sevrl] – *mehrere,* [8]to carry on [ˌkæri‿'ɒn] – *weitermachen*

Green Line 5
ISBN: 978-3-12-547164-1

Unit 3 Media-mad

1 Listening: Modern comedy

Text:
So I'm sitting in the bus listening to these two teenage girls behind me. At first I've got no idea what they are talking about, but they both seem to be very popular and well-liked young women. I mean, I hear them talking about meeting three new people on Thursday, eight on Friday (weekends are best for meeting new people) and twelve more the rest of the weekend. I think, wow, I must be doing something wrong. I meet my newspaper boy in the morning when I can't sleep, but it's always the same newspaper boy. And I ... well, I really don't meet anyone new. I must be hanging out in the wrong places and stuff. Then one of the girls says that after last weekend she made her first hundred. And I think, wait a minute! Meeting new people, making her first hundred. Are these the kinds of girls I think they might be? Are they talking about what I think they're talking about? I decide to steal a look at them and see if I am right. So I slowly turn my head and act like I'm reading the advertisement on the wall next to them. As I turn my head back, I quickly look at both of them and decide that no, these are not ladies of the night. Then the other girl says, "Wait, let me count mine. I've got 108 friends now!" "Cool!" says the other girl. Friends. Friends ... One hundred friends. I know that I do not have 100 friends. If I invited everyone I knew to my next birthday party, I would not have 100 friends. And I'm older than these girls. I've lived in different cities. I've got a job – well, if you can call what I'm doing up here on this stage a job. But I do not have 100 friends. And while I'm thinking about my less than 100 friends, I hear some beeping and peeping from the girls next to me. And they're playing with their cell phones, their mobiles, their cells. Their cells aren't much bigger than their hand. I didn't know they made communication toys that little. Before you laugh at me, yes – I do own a cell phone. But mine is not much bigger than the wheel of my car. It's an older model – my cell and my car. Well, these girls are pushing buttons on their cells, but they are not speaking with anyone. Suddenly one of the girls says, "Hey! Another friend. Look! That means I'm at 101!" I reach into my bag and feel my wheel-sized cell. Are there friends in my cell, too? Are they just waiting for me to find them? Is that where I can meet people and make friends? "What's his name?" the other girl asks about friend 101. "Ummm, I think it's a she. But I didn't see her name. I'll check later if we chat," girl one answers. She doesn't know her friend's name. She thinks it's a girl – but isn't sure. I guess I would have trouble remembering 101 names, too. Suddenly I feel very lucky and not even a little jealous that I've only got a few friends. I know if they're men or women, I know their names and I even know most of their birthdays and get invited, too. And even if I exchange my wheel-sized cell for one of those hand-sized ones, I still won't have 101 friends.

a) 1. B; 2. C; 3. B; 4. C

b) 1. A; 2. C; 3. C; 4. A; 5. A; 6. B; 7. C; 8. B

2 Understanding films: Starting a new job

1. Maya says hello in German./She wants to see the head of reception.
2. Her name is Nicole Schmidt./She speaks English well./She tells Maya to improve her German skills.
3. The caller's last name is Xiao.

3 Reading: The chance of her life

a) A5, B3, C2, D1, E6, F4

b) (1) Yes! (2) The situation changes (3) The offer (4) Dreaming (5) Different opinions about holidays (6) Talking business

c) 1. Carolyn; 2. Hendrik Benson; 3 Robert S. Halmond; 4. Hendrik Benson; 5. Robert S. Halmond; 6. Carolyn; 7. Robert S. Halmond; 8. Carolyn

4 Writing: Soaps!

Individuelle Lösungen

5 Speaking: My use of media

Individuelle Vorträge

6 Mediation: An interview

1. *Seit sie ungefähr zwölf war, liebte sie Filme und Videos und mit 14 fragte sie in der Schule den Berufsberater danach.*
2. *Ihre Mutter ist Chinesin.*
3. *Sie studierte Film an der Westminster-Universität. Dort hat sie viele Kurzfilme und Videos gedreht.*
4. *Nein, denn zuerst gibt es Besprechungen und dann muss das Drehbuch geschrieben werden.*
5. *Bei kurzen Werbefilmen sieht man schneller ein Ergebnis.*
6. *Sie macht sich manchmal Sorgen um die Zukunft, weil sie freiberuflich arbeitet. Sie muss also immer nach neuen Aufträgen suchen.*
7. *Sie will aber bis dahin in Amerika sein, weil dort die Filmbedingungen besser sind.*

Green Line 5
ISBN: 978-3-12-547164-1

7 Inversion: An e-mail to an agony aunt

only now have I decided, Not only does she come, Only then does she return, not for a moment did I think, Never in my life have I been

8 Emphasis: Going to the cinema

I am, did ask, it's … that, himself, did say, myself, extremely, do hope, What, only is it, herself, it's … that's, itself

9 Simple form – progressive form

haven't been playing, was doing, 've just started, 'm having, need, came, was looking, believe, were playing, is shining, haven't been, 've been, was, 've heard, 've been standing, didn't you tell

10 Revision: Present and past forms

have you ever been, haven't been there yet, 've been thinking, Have you been, went, stayed, did you see, visited, had always wanted, were made, have been, took, show, haven't had, promise, are finished

11 Find the missing words

1. cover; 2. track; 3. television; 4. wide; 5. viewer; 6. inversion

12 Definitions

1. the place where something, for example information, comes from
2. what people say about other people behind their backs
3. words in a commercial which the readers/viewers can remember easily
4. to make music in the street
5. a shot in films which shows a face/person from just a few centimetres away
6. to tell a story in a few words

13 Adjectives from participles

developed, given, animated, designed, known, finished, visited, downloaded

14 ⟨How a song is made⟩

listen, melody, recording, vocals, tracks, edit out, sound effects, promote, charts

15 How to: Argue politely

Lösungsvorschlag:

J: I downloaded a few songs from the Internet yesterday.
D: Downloading songs from the Internet is often illegal.
J: They needn't put new songs on the net. Then people wouldn't download them.
D: You don't know who put it there. It's like stealing the artist's money.
J: I don't care about the artist. The record company will pay him anyway.
D: They won't have enough money if all the songs are downloaded illegally.
J: Then they should make the CDs cheaper so that you don't have to do it.
D: You may have to pay a lot of money if they find out. At least use a legal download source, even if it costs some money!

16 Mixed bags

a) as, whether/if, So, to, As, Although, with, Because, at, But, so, in, Since/As, for

b) didn't have, have, has been, was, wanted, had to do, has to go, will have

Zusätzlicher Text für das Hörverstehen:
A new reality show – Division of Labor[1]

Interviewer: Good morning and welcome to WKIT. This is Jennifer Carlson and you're listening to "Media Rap". Today on the show I'm talking to Nathan Baer, who has a new idea for a reality show. Nathan, do you enjoy watching reality TV?

Nathan: I don't watch a lot of reality TV. When it first started it was new and unique so I watched a few shows. In the last few years I haven't watched a lot since many of the shows are almost the same.

Interviewer: You've come up with an idea for a new reality TV show. But don't you think there are already enough of those shows on the market?

Nathan: There are definitely too many of the same type of reality shows on TV. The challenge is to come up with something new. We've all seen the basic reality TV show that has been on for the last 7–10 years. I'm tired of watching those types of shows and I think that I have come up with something different that people will really enjoy.

Interviewer: So there's room for yet another show in your opinion. What makes your show different from the shows that are already on TV?

Green Line 5
ISBN: 978-3-12-547164-1

Nathan: Most of the shows on TV right now are empty, without any meaning. My show idea is not only different, but the plan is to give useful advice to couples[2] who might be having problems with sharing jobs in the house.

Interviewer: Can you explain the show to us?

Nathan: My name for the show is "Division of Labor", which means sharing jobs. Often people feel that they are doing more work than their partner. The idea of the show is to allow people to see the other side. Maybe the other person is doing just as much work, cleaning the house, taking care of the kids or washing the clothes. The show will give points to each of the jobs and will help to make things the same. I hope that the end result is that partners become stronger and that each partner realizes better what the other does.

Interviewer: How did you come up with the idea?

Nathan: I go to lunch once a week with my best friend. We have both been married about nine years. Many times at lunch we would criticize our wives because the house wasn't cleaned or organized and we would list all of the things that we do to keep the house organized AND work more than 40 hours per week. The conversation would always come back to all of the things that our wives did and how difficult they are. So we didn't need to do so much criticizing because after we realistically looked at the situation we had a deeper understanding of what our wives do.

Interviewer: Would you, or rather you and your wife, take part in this show?

Nathan: Definitely, we are the perfect couple and have the perfect division of labor in our home so it might be boring on TV. That, of course, is a joke. I know that my wife still feels that she does more and I feel that I do more.

Interviewer: Why do you think reality shows are so popular?

Nathan: Many of the reality shows on TV today are about negative things. And the people who watch like to be able to say that they are better than the people on TV. There might be some good in that. Most people can find a link to reality TV and if they can't they will say, "Thank God I'm not as bad as those people."

Interviewer: Do people really believe they'll become famous? Are five minutes or 30 minutes or two hours on TV really worth showing people your private life?

Nathan: I'm not really sure what moves people. It may be the idea that they can make some fast money if they are on a show like this. There are definitely many examples of that happening in the US. On my show I see people taking part who are having real problems with their partner. I really believe that people can improve their relationships[3] and families by taking part. One of the best ways to have an influence on big groups of people is by showing them on TV that this can work.

Interviewer: Thank you, Nathan. We wish you the best of luck and maybe we'll see your name on TV someday.

[1]division of labour [dɪˌvɪʒn‿əv ˈleɪbə] – *Arbeitsteilung,* [2]couple [ˈkʌpl] – *Paar,* [3]relationship [rɪˈleɪʃnʃɪp] – *Beziehung*

Zusätzlicher Text für das Leseverstehen:
Wikipedia – pros and cons of the online encyclopaedia[1]

Pros:

I think that Wikipedia is one of the best things on the Internet. There are articles on almost any subject you can think of. In fact[2], in 2007 the English version of Wikipedia reached the mark of two million articles. That makes it the largest encyclopaedia ever! So if you're looking for information on a subject, this is a good place to get a general idea of it and there are often links, too. It's very fast and easy to find the information using the 'search' button. That means, for example, if you don't understand something at school, Wikipedia can give you a quick answer and show you where else you can look.

For pupils it's also very important that Wikipedia is free. It's available to everyone. You don't have to pay anything if you download a picture or copy some of the text. There aren't even any ads on it like on many search engines so you don't get distracted while you're researching a subject.

Wikipedia is also available in many different languages. This helps with translating, for example. And because people all around the world use it, you get lots of different kinds of information. Anyone can edit[3] an article or add a new article. It's good that it's an open project and not just for an elite group.

Usually the information is up-to-date[4] so you can use Wikipedia for news, too. Sometimes it's faster than the news on TV or in newspapers.

Cons:

I think that Wikipedia is one of the worst things that has happened to the Internet. People believe that everything they find there is true. This is a big problem because anybody can edit the articles and they can put in false information. This information stays in until someone else changes it again and so it can spread[5] very quickly through the Internet. When you read an article, you can't be sure that everything is correct. And because maybe

Green Line 5
ISBN: 978-3-12-547164-1

many different people helped to write an article, the writing style is not always good. Wikipedia isn't controlled enough.
There also aren't enough sources given so you don't always know where the authors got their information from. This also means that the articles can be very one-sided. Wikipedia cannot give a guarantee that the information is neutral. There have been times when people were offered money to 'clean up' Wikipedia articles. Politicians might have people change the article about them and take out any critical or negative comments.
Because Wikipedia is so fast and has new information, people depend[6] even more on the Internet. They don't take the time to check any other sources. Often information from Wikipedia is copied and used and the source is not given. This is wrong because you always have to say where you got your information from.

[1]encyclopeadia [ɪnˌsaɪkləˈpiːdɪə] – *Lexikon,* [2]in fact [ɪn ˈfækt] – *tatsächlich,* [3]to edit [ˈedɪt] – *bearbeiten,* [4]up-to-date [ˌʌptəˈdeɪt] – *aktuell,* [5]to spread [spred] – *sich verbreiten,* [6]to depend on [dɪˈpend‿ɒn] – *abhängen von*

Unit 4 Human rights

1 Listening: The freedom of the press

Text:
When well-known Member of Parliament Paul Smith opened a magazine yesterday evening, he was shocked. The first page featured a big photograph of him and his wife on their wedding day, outside a church. In the article about the event, the complete guest list was printed, and one could also read all about the food served that day. Smith, however, had not invited anybody from the media to his wedding. How could all this information now be in the paper? he wondered. Smith decided to phone the magazine's editor, Larry Miller, to complain about the situation.

LM: Larry Miller speaking.
PS: Hello, this is Paul Smith. I opened up your magazine last night and discovered my wedding photograph on the first page – where did you get the photo from?
LM: One of my reporters took it, Mr Smith. You know, you can't have an article about an MP getting married and not have a wedding photo!
PS: But there were no reporters at my wedding, and I didn't agree to any article or photos being printed about the event.
LM: Oh, I know that. But why do you think we should ask you when we inform our readers about your wedding? The people need to know what is happening in their MP's life, don't they?
PS: Well, no. I feel you've taken away my right to privacy with the article and photograph.
LM: Speaking of rights: what about the British people's right to information, and what about the freedom of the press then? The right to information is considered to be one of the most important rights, if not the most important right, in a democracy. Only informed citizens can make good decisions. How can people form their opinions without information?
PS: I still don't see why this means people have to know so much about my wedding. We chose a small castle in the Scottish Highlands for the wedding, hoping for some privacy. You could at least have asked me for permission to print both the article and the photograph. But why should anyone need to know who I invited to my wedding and what food was served? I don't think this information has anything to do with my position as an MP.
LM: You're forgetting the freedom of the press, my friend. We – the press – have a duty to report to the people of Britain what is happening in the UK and the world; people need to feel informed. But if there are too many limits on what the press can do, then how can we help the public to feel informed? I'm sorry, but the personal feelings of one person can't be as important as giving the people of a whole country information.

Green Line 5
ISBN: 978-3-12-547164-1

PS: But it's not news! It's a wedding! And if I had wanted any photographs of my wedding printed, I'd have accepted one of the offers to sell our wedding story to a different magazine, not to yours! But now that the article and the photo have already been printed, I suggest that you pay me what I was offered for the story by the other magazines.

LM: I'm sorry, Mr Smith. You're a public person, and you were standing outside a church, in public, when the photo was taken. Why should I pay for that?

PS: Fine. My lawyer will be phoning your lawyer. This could be expensive for you.

a) Pictures 1, 4, 7, 8

b) 1. a Member of Parliament; 2. guests, food; 3. one of Larry Smith's reporters; 4. the right to privacy; 5. good decisions; 6. in a small castle/in the Scottish Highlands; 7. the freedom of the press; 8. to sell his wedding story; 9. Paul Smith is a public person./The photo was taken in public.

2 Understanding films: Facing challenges

1. I need a table at the Four Seasons.
2. I have no idea how to make a reservation.
3. The Four Seasons is booked out tonight.
4. Leave a message on my cell phone.
5. Do you think I'm stupid?
6. I'll take care of your Internet.

3 Reading: Stop and search

a) 2. lines 5–6; 3. lines 6–7; 4. line 11; 5. lines 15–17; 6. lines 20–21; 7. line 26; 8. lines 29–30; 9. lines 32–33

b) 1 Jack walks home. 2 The policemen stop Jack. 3 Jack asks the officers to let him pass. 4 One of the officers empties Jack's pockets while the other one holds his arms. 5 Jack wakes up with his arms hurting. 6 Jack talks to the social worker.

4 Writing: A newspaper article

Lösungsvorschlag:

This is the story of Jack Davies who is 29 years old and was born in our town. He went to high school here and is now working in an office in the town center. He has friends, does sports and goes out to discos and restaurants. Sounds like a normal life, doesn't it? But it's not! Jack Davies is black and therefore is, in some police officers' eyes at least, a possible drug dealer. While walking home last week, he was stopped in the street by two police officers who wanted him to empty his pockets. When Jack asked why, they told him that he was suspected of being a member of a gang of drug dealers. As Jack had never broken the law in his whole life, he refused. That's when one of the officers grabbed his arms and held them tightly while his partner searched Jack's pockets for drugs. Of course they didn't find any. After they had dropped all of Jack's things on the ground, the police officers left without a word. Is this normal? Is this how black people are treated in our town? Has anything like that happened to you? Send your story in and we'll let everybody know!

5 Speaking: Human rights

Individuelle Vorträge

6 Mediation: An important figure of the human rights movement

Martin Luther King was born in 1929. He was one of the most famous human rights activists in the US. His biggest goal in life was the fight against segregation. Under his leadership, the blacks fought for and won the right to vote, and they were able to stop segregation, for example at schools. It was always important to King that protest was peaceful. In 1963 he led a protest march to Washington and gave a great speech. 250,000 people went with him. He had a lot of enemies even inside the movement because many people thought that they should use violence to achieve their goals. In 1968, when he was only 39 years old, King was shot. But King's dream of a society without racism is still alive today.

7 Fill in the right prepositions

in, to, to, without, to, about, with, of, for, about, to, into, with

8 Gerund or infinitive

to live, to speak, criticizing, to support, to enter, to get, getting into, thinking, to stop

9 Verbs

1. to be; 2. to going; 3. being; 4. going; 5. thinking; 6. to understand; 7. to hurt, saying; 8. (to) become

10 Indirect speech

Jack told me that he had been on his way home when the policemen had stopped him without any obvious reason. He had been asked to take off his cap and empty his pockets.
I asked him how many policemen had been there.

Green Line 5
ISBN: 978-3-12-547164-1

He said that there had been two of them and that they had been very rude. When Jack had not done as he had been told, one of them had grabbed his arms and the other one had taken his cap and (had) thrown everything Jack had had in his pockets on the ground.
I asked Jack if they had told them why he had been stopped and searched.
Jack told me that he hadn't been told (anything) until he had asked. Then the police officers told Jack he had been suspected of being a member of a gang of drug dealers. But as I knew him, he would never have done that kind of thing. The policemen had only let go of him after they had realized he hadn't been carrying any drugs. Jack said that he had now really lost confidence in the police.

11 Modals and their substitutes

had to, Weren't you able/allowed to/Couldn't you, had to, wasn't allowed to, did you have to, wasn't able, were allowed to, weren't allowed to, couldn't, had to, will be able to

12 How to: Show everyday courage and support

Individuelle Lösungen

13 Crossword

Across: 5. integration; 8. segregation; 9. gay; 10. protest; 12. homeless
Down: 1. congress; 2. crime; 3. democracy; 4. freedom; 6. racism; 7. slavery; 11. tolerate

14 Phrases

1. to change your mind; 2. to complain to the waiter; 3. to handle a problem; 4. to make a difference; 5. to pass a law; 6. to qualify as perfect; 7. to receive a good education; 8. to recruit soldiers; 9. to ban child labour; 10. to tolerate a different opinion

15 Mixed bag: Human rights

democratic, equal, developing world, to integrate, In spite of, appropriate, position of power, slavery, target, considered to, child labour, bullied, dignity, improve, speak out about, attention

Zusätzlicher Text für das Hörverstehen:
The United Nations conference against racism
20–24 April, 2009 in Geneva, Switzerland

Reporter: I've just heard from our reporter inside the conference that the President of Iran Ahmadinejad is giving a speech at this moment. President Ahmadinejad is the reason that many countries, like the United States, Germany and Israel, decided not to come to the UN conference here in Geneva, Switzerland. I've just been told that many people are leaving the room – those representing Great Britain and France and other countries. They're standing up and walking out during President Ahmadinejad's speech. They're protesting against what they call his racist comments about Israel. President Ahmadinejad said that a racist government was set up in Palestine – Israel.
Let's listen to what some of the people here outside of the conference think about this.
Excuse me, what do you think about President Ahmadinejad speaking at the UN conference on racism?

Man 1: You can't talk to a man like Ahmadinejad. He's using this conference to spread hate and not to get rid of it. That's what they want to achieve at this conference. He doesn't want to make any changes. He doesn't want to listen.

Reporter: And what do you think about the countries that did not come to the conference?

Man 1: I'm not sure …

Woman 1: I'll tell you what I think. Those countries should be here! They need to help. Everyone is focusing on Ahmadinejad now. The important countries like the US are not here. They could have shown the world that they are against racism. But they didn't come so this means the fight against racism has been delayed again.

Man 1: But I think they did make a strong statement by not coming. Like I said, you can't talk to someone like Ahmadinejad. And if the important countries are not here to listen to his lies, then that's a strong signal. He's not worth our time.

Reporter: But if all of the UN members do not take part, then how can the UN fight racism?

Man 2: Ahmadinejad is the only world leader who accepted the invitation to the conference. If the other countries were serious about fighting racism, they would send their presidents and prime ministers[1]. The word here is "fight". How can Obama fight racism if he's at home and Ahmadinejad is here? How can Germany support Israel if the chancellor[2] is at home and Ahmadinejad is here? The UN will never have a real plan if all countries don't take part and help.

Man 1: But Ahmadinejad wants the UN to say that it is wrong to criticize any religion. The UN can't do that. What about the freedom of speech?

[1]prime minister [ˌpraɪm‿ˈmɪnɪstə] – *Pemierminister/in*,
[2]chancellor [ˈtʃɑːnslə] – *Kanzler/in*

Green Line 5
ISBN: 978-3-12-547164-1

Zusätzlicher Text für das Leseverstehen:
A child of the 'Stolen Generation' – A short biography

Archie Roach was born in 1956 in Mooroopna, Australia. As a small child he lived in a mission house and later with foster[1] parents, the Coxes, in Melbourne. At the time Roach was too small to remember his past but, in fact[2], he wasn't a real orphan[3]: He was a child of the so-called 'Stolen Generation' (see Info).

In Melbourne, Roach learned to play the guitar and the keyboard from Mary, the Coxes' oldest daughter. He loved music. The family were Scottish immigrants and they had lots of records, so he heard different music styles.

One day, when Roach was older, he got a letter from one of his sisters. She told him about what had happened to their family when the children were small. He was so angry about the lies the foster family had told him that he left the Coxes' home. He wanted to find the other members of his real family. But his parents had died and the only member he ever saw again was one of his sisters. With only his guitar in his hand, he travelled to Sydney and Adelaide. Of course, he had no money so he lived out in the streets. It was a difficult time in his life and he drank a lot. This was also when he began to make his own music and met his future partner, Ruby Hunter, who was a musician, too. At the end of 1980 Roach and Hunter started a band, the 'Altogethers'.

One of Roach's first songs was called 'Took the Children Away'. It was about his own past. But it was more than that: It told the story of the Native Australian people's fight for their rights, including[4] the right to land and to their own family. It moved many Australians across the country, both Native and white, when he played it on a TV show.

Roach became known all around the world in the year of the Olympics in Sydney (2000) when 'Time Magazine' did an article about him and put his photo on the cover.

Today Roach and Hunter live with their children near Berri, South Australia. They keep their home open to Native Australian kids and offer them a break from life out on the street.

INFO: The Stolen Generation

Aborigines are to Australia what Native Americans are to the US. They were the first people who lived there. Between 1869 and 1969 tens of thousands of Aborigine children (the 'Stolen Generation') were taken from their parents by white officials[5]. The kids were taken to missions where they were very unhappy and missed their families. They were taught to pray[6] and then they were sent to foster homes where they often had to do all the housework.

[1]foster ['fɒstə] – *Pflege-*, [2]in fact [ɪn 'fækt] – *tatsächlich*,
[3]orphan ['ɔ:fn] – *Waise*, [4]including [ɪn'klu:dɪŋ] – *einschließlich*,
[5]official [ə'fɪʃl] – *Beamter/Beamtin*, [6]to pray [preɪ] – *beten*

Green Line 5
ISBN: 978-3-12-547164-1

Hörverstehenstexte zu den Standardaufgaben

Track	Unit	Text/Übungstitel	Seite	Übung	Spielzeit
1	1	Listening: Australian crocodiles	7	1	2'48"
2	1	Listening: Henry is visiting Edward in Australia	52	Zusatz	2'50"
3	2	Listening: Careers talk	19	1	3'47"
4	2	Listening: A job interview for practice	55–56	Zusatz	4'17"
5	3	Listening: Modern comedy	30	1	4'53"
6	3	Listening: A new reality show – Division of Labour	58–59	Zusatz	4'40"
7	4	Listening: The freedom of the press	40	1	4'10"
8	4	Listening: The UN conference against racism ...	62	Zusatz	3'19"

Gesamtspielzeit: 30'43"

Lehrersoftware-CD

Empfohlene Systemvoraussetzungen:

- PC mit 500 MHz oder höher
- Windows 2000, XP, Vista (32 bit)
- 128 MB RAM
- S-VGA-kompatible Grafikkarte mit 16,7 Mio Farben (24 bit)
- mind. 50 MB bis max. 300 MB freier Speicherplatz bei Kopie der Medien auf die Festplatte
- 24fach CD-ROM-Laufwerk
- Bildschirmauflösung (Programm) 800 x 600 Pixel
- Schwarzweiß- oder Farbdrucker mit 300 dpi Druckauflösung
- Microsoft Word (ab Version 2000) oder OpenOffice (ab Version 2.0)

Abspiel-Umgebungen und Datei-Betrachter für die Medien befinden sich auf der CD-ROM.

Schnellstart der Software:

Die Installation kopiert das Programm auf die Festplatte Ihres Rechners. Wir empfehlen, die Medien sofort auf die Festplatte zu installieren. Sie brauchen dann die CD-ROM nicht mehr einzulegen, um das Programm zu verwenden.

- Legen Sie die Lehrersoftware CD in Ihr CD-ROM-Laufwerk ein.
- Die Autostartfunktion öffnet ein Fenster mit dem Inhalt der CD-ROM.
- Starten Sie die Datei „SETUP.EXE" durch Doppelklick und folgen Sie den Anweisungen, um das Programm und die Medien auf Ihre Festplatte zu installieren.
- Um das Programm zu installieren, müssen Sie dem Lizenzvertrag zustimmen (s.a. **Lizenz.txt** auf der CD-ROM).
- Den Pfad für die Programminstallation auf der Festplatte können Sie anpassen oder nach der Vorgabe übernehmen.
- Sie starten das Programm über Start – Programme – Klett – Green Line – Lehrersoftware Green Line oder über das Icon auf Ihrem Desktop.

Auf der CD-ROM befindet sich ein ausführliches Handbuch zum Programm.